"This book is exactly what is ne
approachable and comprehensiv
—*Ginger Healy, Program Director, Attachment & Trauma Network*

"A richly resourced gift to our children and ourselves. A call to action for parents, teachers, and professors to administrators and government. The trauma informed framework integrates ground-breaking insights from neuroscience to social justice. Read it. Gift it."

—*Dr. Brenda Morrison, Director, Research and Engagement
Centre for Restorative Justice, Simon Fraser University*

"The neurodevelopmental basis for behavior, the impact of trauma and it's accomplice shame, and the restorative approach are integrated into a practical and applicable framework and guide for the creation of healthy classrooms where children can thrive."

—*Rick Kelly, M.Sc, Executive Director,
Just Us: A Centre for Restorative Practices*

"What a great book! It really confirmed the work and direction we have taken with our schools and staff in Whethersfield, while allowing me to reflect on next steps and big shifts in culture that are occurring! When every educator embraces these ideas every learner in the school benefits immensely! I can only imagine the work you have put into this book to capture all of the nuances, references and latest research! Lots to be proud of!"

—*Sally Dastoli, Assistant Superintendent of Schools for
Curriculum and Instruction, Wethersfield Public Schools*

"Wow! This book is a rich tapestry of theory and neuroscience, illustrated in accessible ways; a practical guidance to implement such learnings in the classroom and beyond' and most importantly it cultivates the relational thinking and motivation needed to engage whole-heartedly with this trauma-informed restorative work! It's a gift for all those working in education, lighting the way for meaningful connection with the self and others. Thank you Joe and Marg—what a dream team you are!"

—*Michelle Stowe, (teacher at heart), founder and director of Connect RP*

"A brave and incisive book, compiling the most recent understanding of the brain and trauma into practical guidance for educators. The explanation of restorative processes underscores the importance of being trauma-informed and restorative, for the sake of us all."

—*Nancy Riestenberg, author of Circle in the Square:
Building Community and Repairing Harm in School*

"This book is a critical call to action for educators. It's time to move beyond rewards and punishment and embrace a trauma-informed, neuroscience-aligned approach to creating a better world for all of us."

—*Guy Stephens, Alliance Against Seclusion and Restraint*

from the same author

Building a Trauma-Informed Restorative School
Skills and Approaches for Improving Culture and Behavior
Joe Brummer with Margaret Thorsborne
Foreword by Judy Atkinson
ISBN 978 1 78775 267 2
eISBN 978 1 78775 268 9

The Continuum of Restorative Practices in Schools
An Instructional Training Manual for Practitioners
Margaret Thorsborne and Dave Vinegrad
Foreword by Brenda Morrison
ISBN 978 1 83997 041 2
eISBN 978 1 83997 042 9

Implementing Restorative Practices in Schools
A Practical Guide to Transforming School Communities
Margaret Thorsborne and Peta Blood
Foreword by Graham Robb
ISBN 978 1 84905 377 8
eISBN 978 0 85700 737 7

of related interest

The A–Z of Trauma-Informed Teaching
Strategies and Solutions to Help with Behaviour
and Support for Children Aged 3–11
*Sarah Naish, Anne Oakley, Hannah O'Brien,
Sair Penna and Daniel Thrower*
ISBN 978 1 83997 205 8
eISBN 978 1 83997 208 9

Raising Kids with Big, Baffling Behaviors
Brain-Body-Sensory Strategies That Really Work
Robyn Gobbel
Foreword by Bonnie Badenoch, PhD
ISBN 978 1 83997 428 1
eISBN 978 1 83997 429 8

BECOMING A TRAUMA-INFORMED RESTORATIVE EDUCATOR

Practical Skills to Change
Culture and Behavior

JOE BRUMMER and
MARGARET THORSBORNE

Foreword by Dr. Lori L. Desautels

Jessica Kingsley Publishers
London and Philadelphia

First published in Great Britain in 2024 by Jessica Kingsley Publishers
An imprint of John Murray Press

1

Printed and bound in the United States by Integrated Books International

Jessica Kingsley Publishers' policy is to use papers that are natural, renewable and recyclable products and made from wood grown in sustainable
forests. The logging and manufacturing processes are expected to conform
to the environmental regulations of the country of origin.

Jessica Kingsley Publishers
Carmelite House
50 Victoria Embankment
London EC4Y 0DZ

www.jkp.com

John Murray Press
Part of Hodder & Stoughton Ltd
An Hachette Company

***Marg:** This book is dedicated to my half-sister Billie (1936–2020), whose beginning in life was deeply compromised by the death of her biological mother, ten days after she was born. My sister grew in her mummy's tummy while her mother was dying. I cannot fathom the grief that would have been transmitted to her in utero, or the disruption she faced when my father married again and she was uplifted from her primary carer, her maternal grandmother, into a new family. I am so sad that I did not know about trauma and its long shadow, or understand her struggles to feel she was worthy of love and belonging. It may have made a difference to both of us.*

***Joe:** None of the work I do would be possible without the love and endless support my husband, Rick Cain, has offered me. Since day one, he has provided me with a space in life to heal from the things that have happened to me. He has proved to me more than anyone that I am loveable, capable, and that I can live up to my potential. With that said, I dedicate this book to him with gratitude for his love and patience with me as I continue to heal every day.*

Contents

Acknowledgements

Writing this book has been a case of agony and ecstasy for me. Perhaps not quite as dramatic as that, but both of us have struggled at times with writer's block and knowing whose work to reference amid a plethora of models (especially how to explain brain structure and function) and other theories about motivation and behavior change. We are driven, as consultant educators (as many of our colleagues are), to help teachers change the way they think, and do, behavior development. It's a source of great delight to meet those who are already thinking this way (or are open to thinking differently) and have done their homework to keep up with modern theories and see the positive results of this in their schools.

From my own perspective, the work of Dr. Bruce Perry, Dr. Lori Desautels, Dr. Ross Greene, Alfie Kohn, Dr. Gabor Maté, and Dr. Vick Kelly has left a permanent impression on how I have come to make sense of the world. Other inspiring work can be found in our extensive reference list. One of the best bits about writing this book is having to read extensively, and I think as a result I might be better at teaching these concepts. I have enjoyed reaching out to a range of practitioners who are doing the practical work around regulation: Meagan Baldwin in the USA, Lindy Anning and Ben Alpas from my home state of Queensland in Australia (look for their stories in the Appendix), and all the others who are doing this work in schools already—you are unsung heroes! What a difference you make.

I would like to honor Joe, my co-author. I knew a little about Joe's work before I met him face to face in Minnesota at a restorative conference in 2018. What followed was a developing relationship as I assisted in getting his first book, *Building a Trauma-Informed Restorative School*, published in 2021. During those first-book efforts and the collaboration for this one, our contact has been necessarily via Zoom or FaceTime. During that time, we have shared stories about our families and lives, as well as professional and theoretical issues. Joe is well acquainted with his own experiences of abuse, neglect, violence, and trauma. I am in awe of everything he has done to overcome these challenges and I have witnessed how this guides his commitment to this important work. I hope he has felt supported to get this book to print. We have both learned such a lot. And I have loved working on this project with you, Joe.

I cannot mention Joe without appreciating his husband Rick Cain. Rick has an eye for detail around the all-important aspect of references, grammar, and general wording. This is the final bit before handing a manuscript over, and for me, utterly tedious. That someone so close to the authors has committed to doing this for us as a labor of love, and somehow finds the task satisfying, is miraculous! His advice, encouragement, and attention to detail have been a gift. Rick, you have saved my sanity.

My own husband, Mick Brown, continues to be the glue that holds me and my work together. He never complains about how much time I spend in front of my computer, how many meetings I attend in person or online, how much time I am away from home for work, or how much of my time is not his to share. I hope he knows I do not take any of that for granted. Joe and Rick have witnessed online his early morning trips out to get my coffee—one of my great joys of life! I could not have done this without him quietly in the background. I am so very grateful.

Marg Thorsborne
September 2023

When we started this book, I had no idea where we were going with it. What we turned out together feels magical. The flow and ideas-sharing with Marg have been amazing. This book and my first are my attempts to create a world where a kid like me would have been okay. There are many people to thank; this little blurb would never cut it. Here are my attempts.

I am starting with Marg. When a 30-year pioneer of this work wants to write a book with you, you do it! I have learned much from

Marg about writing and the thinking that makes this work possible. It is an honor to co-author a book with someone with such experience and wisdom to offer all of us. A nod to our mutual friend, Lee Rush, for introducing us, and Mick Brown for putting up with all our Zooms and supplying the coffee.

A thank you to every educator who allowed me into their classrooms, schools, or districts. I learn so much from you! I would not be doing this had you all not been a part of my journey at one point or another.

Aside from teaching me that nothing is wrong with me and my brain just got hijacked by what happened to me, Dr. Bruce Perry generously allowed me to attend his Neurosequential Model in Education (NME) Training Certification Program to dive deeper into his work. That training and his work have greatly influenced this book. He also allowed Marg and me to use his graphics to help us talk about his work. I am truly grateful for his gifts to this work and his influence on helping me heal from my trauma. I add to this the works of Gabor Maté, Daniel Siegel, Ginger Healy, Mona Delahooke, Resmaa Menakem, Nadine Burke Harris, Lisa Feldman Barrett, Ross Greene, Fania Davis, Dorothy Vaandering, Kay Pranis, Carolyn Boyes-Watson, Kathy Evans, Stacey Patton, and so many others who have helped me build this knowledge.

A special thank you to Dr. Lori Desautels for her kindness and support of my work, and for writing the foreword of this book. Further special gratitude goes to amazing friends and colleagues Meg Baldwin and Jessica Harris for contributing their wisdom to this book, constantly supporting me, and being there every time I send a text.

I am grateful to my trauma-informed chat group, a cheering section of people who never seem to stop believing in me, and amazing trauma experts doing life-changing stuff in the world. Our chat group keeps me regulated through relational rewards. Thank you, Stacy Nation, Kerrie Ackerson, James Moffett, Matthew Portell, Jodi Place, Dustin Springer, Lara Kain, Jim Sporleader, Tracie Chavin, and Briana Kurlinkus. Add to this list my friends at the Attachment and Trauma Network who have also supported me.

Gratitude to my sister, Chris. We survived so much together, and we are learning to heal together. I am forever amazed by you, proud of you, and grateful to have you in my life.

There is a reason I dedicated this book to my husband, Rick. He is amazing, and without him, nothing I have could exist. Thank you for just always being there for me, and thank you for loving me.

Joe Brummer
September 2023

Foreword

Joe and Margaret have collaborated to produce a superb new book containing a body of translatable knowledge, guidance, and practices addressing how trauma and adversity impact the developing nervous system. They have explored the power and complexity inside the applications of brain and body-aligned restorative repair and growth interventions through a personal, professional, and social equity journey.

When you share a conversation with Marg and Joe, their passion and commitment to this work spills out in such honest and authentic discussions. They embody their words, beliefs, and perceptions. They are so very intentional about dismantling the punitive practices that can often contribute to the racial and neurodivergent disparities and disproportionalities we are experiencing in our schools as we address trauma, behaviors, discipline, and relational regulation. The post-pandemic environments felt and experienced in our schools are exacerbating the conditions. Joe and Marg embrace these challenges through this new book. In their words from the section entitled "The invitation" in Chapter 7:

> In a general sense, the restorative approach involves a sequence that usually begins with an invitation to see the process as *an opportunity to make sense of what happened* rather than to lay blame or sit in judgment of the people in the problem, whether or not they might be good or bad, or to tell them off. It attempts to understand what harm has happened, and how that harm might be addressed. There is agency/autonomy in this approach—students and young people participate voluntarily (some, to be sure, reluctantly at first), and we need to be genuinely invitational in our approach.

"Invitational" is a foundational concept in effective and sustainable restorative practices, as all children and youth experience several small potential traumas during each day and, as trauma therapist and author Bonnie Badenoch suggests, "these shards of accumulating experiences that linger in our muscles, belly, hearts, brains, and body systems gradually shape our perceptual systems and how the world looks" (2018, p.13). Referring to these events as "small traumas" is not intended to diminish or disrespect the horrific experiences so many youth carry into our schools. This research helps us to understand that when we hold the sacred space of co-regulation for our children and youth, we are helping them, through the safety of our own regulated nervous system, to digest and integrate the dysregulating experiences they have amassed. Our brains are complex historical organs with the inherent capacity to self-organize and self-regulate. Still, in many cases, it requires a relational experience to realize this state fully. Each moment with a child is a potentially therapeutic moment. As Dr. Steve Porges (2021) beautifully states, "We wear our hearts on our faces and in our voices, as our nervous systems influence our body's moment-to-moment expression, automatically offering a sense of safety or danger on one another."

Our current understanding of relational, interpersonal neurobiology brings us to a crossroads where this body of knowledge is at the core of how we can re-envision discipline practices and protocols in our schools. Recent research emphasizes that true discipline for our students begins with an adult brain that feels safe, calm, and steady. The behaviors to which we should give the most attention are the behaviors that we want to sprout and flourish. This intentional attention begins with adults willing to dive into their uncontested and possibly unexplored perspectives and belief systems—individual, familial, communal, and generational. These are the perspectives and belief systems we have unintentionally carried into this moment; we should examine them with the intention of doing what is best for our students.

May you find personal and professional grace within this book, written to acknowledge and share a renewed focus on how adult well-being and invitational repairing are the cornerstones to punitive and often re-traumatizing discipline practices. This discipline shift will inform future nervous system-aligned and relational discipline policies. In the compelling words of Dr. Bruce Perry:

> The most traumatic aspects of all disasters involve the shattering of human connections. And this is especially true for children. Being harmed by the people who are supposed to love you, being abandoned by them, being robbed of the one-on-one relationships that allow you to feel safe and valued and to become humane—these are profoundly destructive experiences. Because humans are inescapably social beings, the worst catastrophes that can befall us inevitably involve relational loss. As a result, recovery from trauma and neglect is also all about relationships—rebuilding trust, regaining confidence, returning to a sense of security, and reconnecting to love. Healing and recovery are impossible—even with the best medications and therapy in the world—without lasting, caring connections to others. (Perry & Szalavitz 2006, pp.231–232)

I am so honored to share the foreword of this book, as Joe and Marg have eloquently provided the framework, practices, and mindsets for all who are intentionally willing to sit beside our children and youth, repairing, healing, and providing the resources through restorative protocols for sustainable emotional, social, and physiological growth.

Lori L. Desautels, Ph.D.

CHAPTER 1

Introduction: Explaining Our Why

Welcome to the journey of becoming a trauma-informed restorative educator. This is a journey that has no specific destination, and it's a journey that has no end. New research about the impact of trauma and stress on brain development in children, young people, and adults means we have to constantly recalibrate and integrate what we thought we knew and what is newly discovered. This journey is just as much about unlearning old ways of understanding and interpreting children's behaviors as it is about learning new ways of *being* with children.

Before we begin this journey together, we want to share our motivation for writing this book. This book is much more a personal reflection about how we *think, do,* and *are* compared to our first book, *Building a Trauma-Informed Restorative School: Skills and Approaches for Improving Culture and Behavior* (Brummer & Thorsborne 2020). We must also acknowledge how tough recent years have been. Life has thrown us some curveballs recently.

The Covid-19 pandemic has had a big impact, leaving a huge mark on the mental, physical, relational, and economic health of our communities, including schools, worldwide. Increases in anxiety, depression, and behavioral issues among student populations have been widely reported in Australia (Australian Institute of Health and Welfare 2021), the United States (Oberg *et al.* 2022), and the United Kingdom (Holt & Murray 2021), leading many to believe we need to come down hard with harsher, punitive responses to get children back in line.

Alongside the pandemic, we have had a fair share of natural

disasters—earthquakes, bushfires, floods, droughts, cyclones, hurricanes, tornadoes, tsunamis, climate change impacts—as well as massacres, civil unrest, and the war in Ukraine, which have layered on top of each other like puff pastry. Even if we are not directly affected, we see these stories daily on the news or read them online or in our newspapers. We witness the fallout of the disruptions, distress, and uncertainty created by these multiple traumas in our relationships, what these disconnections do, and how they show up in altered behaviors of our own and others. And this raises a number of questions:

- How do we respond to these behaviors?

- What conclusions do we draw about these altered behaviors?

- What are we seeing in our schools?

- Are we blaming the students, their families, school leadership, and colleagues?

- Do our policies and practices serve us well to find solutions?

- What needs to change?

Doug Lemov, author of *Teach Like a Champion 3.0: 63 Techniques That Put Students on the Path to College* (2021), writes in his latest book, *Reconnect: Building School Culture for Meaning, Purpose, and Belonging* (Lemov *et al.* 2023), that there are three unprecedented problems faced by young people right now:

- A mental health crisis amid the increasing use of screen time, including smartphones, which has profoundly changed the nature of social interactions among young people.

- An increasing lack of trust in institutions, as citizens perceive them as incompetent and lacking in ethical behavior, resulting in increased skepticism and challenge by parents about whether or not schools can educate their children effectively.

- Increasing individualism (as opposed to collectivism), which is costing us a sense of community and mutual obligation in institutions like schools built on social contracts.

We seem to have lost the village.

While it is easy to see why we would fall back on old beliefs in times of high stress, the science is clear that that will only worsen our current situation. In explaining our reasons for writing this book, we hope that some ideas you will meet here will convince you of the need to change what you think and do and how you do it. Also, that it will motivate you with a desire to work differently, to improve what's happening in your classroom (or indeed your relationships beyond school), to get on board with what the school may be asking of you, and to embrace a whole-school approach to trauma-informed and restorative practice. It may also improve your wellness and well-being.

We want to help you take the bit between your teeth and experiment and develop your practice, even knowing this text is no substitute for professional development workshops where we can practice with each other. We hope that you have colleagues who might be reading these words and are willing to process these collective learnings with you. We also want you to know how to sustain your practice—how to be reflective about it, keep your skills current, and avoid slippage, even when you may be one of the few in your school who wants badly to do this kind of work, which can be lonely.

Too many schools proclaim their "restorative-ness" and their "trauma-informed-ness" like some badge without actually translating these proclamations into action, and so, like a spray tan that comes off in the shower, nothing sticks. A one-day professional development training at the start of the school year or a 90-minute twilight session after an exhausting school day does not cut it! Or worse, some schools believe that if we graft humane practices like trauma-informed or restorative approaches onto a deeply rooted retributive tree, with little examination or analysis of this root system, student behavior will be magically transformed. The other phrase we often hear in conversations at training is "I need more tools to know how to make kids behave," which indicates that notions of the quick fix still capture the school.

There are schools still steeped in the past, with a sliding scale of punitive measures to match the seriousness of non-compliant behaviors in and out of the classroom. They are caught in some time warp. This is truly frightening, and it's clear that recent research into brain and behavior development has not yet reached the profession in enough schools—large and small, elementary and high, rural and urban, private and government funded. We cannot believe that this is still happening.

What is needed is to change *adult behavior* in the school to reflect these new understandings about the lives and skills of our students. Equally important, this is also about our own lives and skills and the impacts these have on the relationships in the school community and beyond, not to mention the awareness and understanding of these issues that may (or may not) be reflected in systems, policies, protocols, and changes in data. The pandemic, if it has any gift, has highlighted that, in fundamental ways, we have got much of what we do wrong. It is now time to rethink teaching and learning, pedagogy, managing relationships, classroom dynamics, and how we respond to challenging behavior. *Claiming* to be restorative or trauma-aware is not enough. It has to be felt and visible.

We strongly believe that restorative approaches are better served by a deep dive into understanding the impact of trauma and stress on the lives of children and ourselves. When our school is truly serious about trauma-informed practice, we need to understand how much more effective our practice will be with restorative approaches, measures, and practices for problem-solving.

To make sense of the vast amount of information about our brains and how this applies to our work as educators, we have created a model—a journey in three parts—starting with us, then our classroom, then the systems in which we work (see Figure 1.1). We hope to convince you of the need to address all three parts of this journey. They are completely intertwined.

The first step in this journey is **personal**. This is a journey of unlearning old ways of seeing ourselves and the children with whom we engage in education. It is about *who we are* and *how we show up* for students and each other. Sadly, for some, at this point in the journey, it is also about understanding our history of trauma and its impact on our nervous systems. It is personal, too, because of the values we choose to live by each day. This is values work, and learning to live by our values allows us to respond to the world with intention and compassion. The important question becomes "Who do I want to be, and what values will I live by in any current situation?"

The second step is a **professional** journey that begins in the classroom, changing the old systems and creating new ones without exclusionary, punitive sanctions, inequity, or trauma ignorance. We can't call ourselves trauma-informed while inflicting trauma or making school a place that perpetuates trauma. This means we must become aware of how we might be doing that. Our classrooms must be set up to allow children's brains to experience more safety cues than threats. Our classrooms must also have a sense of belonging for our students.

The third step of this journey is a **social justice** journey. We must do what we can to prevent trauma in our systems, policies, and protocols, and these harms being perpetuated in our communities. We must learn to respond to collective traumas and work toward healing the damage and harm they cause. This means intentionally and explicitly working to end racism, homophobia, sexism, gender violence, and other forms of collective trauma.

We ask you to reflect on how the topics explored can be applied to each of the three pathways in this profound, game-changing journey.

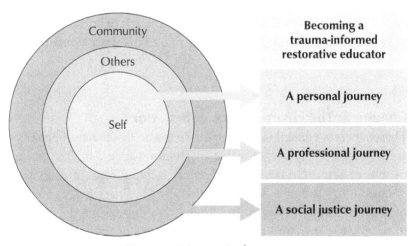

Figure 1.1: A journey in three parts

CHAPTER SUMMARIES

Subsequent chapters are laid out in the following sequence that we hope makes sense. You may choose to chapter-hop in a non-linear way. What pulls at you when you read the table of contents page?

We hope we have cross-referenced other chapters in this book enough to help you navigate this way. We hope you feel challenged and reassured along the way, much like we were (and still are) when confronted with new ideas in this journey.

Chapter 2: A Starting Point: Some Theory, Concepts, and Definitions

This is where the challenges start! We first explore the ubiquitous behaviorism approach to discipline issues and whether or not this now outdated but mostly unchallenged way of managing compliance issues is effective. This allows us to understand the long-term impacts on school policy and practice of a behaviorist mindset, its programs, and its failure to deliver effective behavior development practices and policies. It challenges our thinking about concepts of discipline—accountability, consequences, punishment and rewards, extrinsic and intrinsic motivation, functional behavior assessments, and the myth of quick fixes. We challenge ourselves to reflect on our biases and, more broadly, how the systems we work in are also biased against those we don't regard as "like us." It defines the essence of restorative and trauma-informed practice—these concepts are explored in chapters later in the book.

Chapter 3: The Neuroscience of Behavior

This chapter is a general introduction to the neuroscience of behavior and behavior change, whether we are thinking about children, young people, or adults (and yes, our behavior). It includes an introduction to our biology as highly social animals and Dr. Bruce Perry's Neurosequential Model of brain development, along with a description of basic structures and functions of key parts of the human brain. We describe the neurobiology of stress, trauma, resilience, and state-dependent functioning. What follows explains why we need to develop responses that regulate, relate, and (only then) reason when we are problem-solving with others, and how emotional contagion can work for or against us in these efforts. Finally, we explore what is involved in developing new habits and the subsequent changes to brain structures and functions: predictability and "use it or lose it."

Chapter 4: Regulation and Co-Regulation

In this chapter, a natural follow-on from the basics about the brain, we start by explaining the concept of regulation and co-regulation as antecedents to self-regulation and what this means for our neurobiology and behaviors. We explore what we mean by regulation and its domains, why we need it to access the brain's higher functions, and why it is important for us to understand how it works in our lives and our students' lives. We describe different types of regulation—bottom-up, top-down, dissociation, and the reliance for some on external means of regulation. We unpack the concept of co-regulation and understanding that young people cannot teach themselves to regulate—we must do it *with them* first. We also explore the need for regulating and relating before reasoning by being curious, not furious, and how the elements of this link to restorative practice.

Chapter 5: Wellness: Improving Our Capacity for Regulation

We make a case for looking after ourselves to manage the challenges of our work, especially when we are connecting with children and young people who have backpacks filled with stressors and whose brains may be so dysregulated that *we* risk becoming unsettled. We describe several ways to think about wellness and its links to our capacity to regulate. We introduce the concept of a body budget, which will help us understand the importance of staying balanced via nutrition, exercise, and sleep. Without this balance, our brains cannot cope with the stress we face working in a school. We finish with thoughts about how we have moved beyond what's healthy in how we live our lives and manage our relationships with a call to action to rethink how we might be with each other.

Chapter 6: Trauma, Adversity, and a Regulated Classroom

Given the title of this book, we have expanded on the material we think is important to know about trauma: how it impacts the brain's capacity to predict, how what is traumatic to someone might not be traumatic to another, and how increasing stress levels impact brain function. We describe resilience from the point of view of how stress is handled and what will help to build resilience in ourselves and our students. We explore relational, brain-helpful ways of bringing regulation into our classrooms and making links using circle and, more generally, relational pedagogy.

Chapter 7: Restorative Approaches: Translating Theory and Principles into Practice

In this chapter, we elaborate on the basics of restorative practice. We cover in more detail the difference between retributive and restorative approaches to problem-solving; the basic philosophy and underlying principles of this different approach to accountability with its focus on harm over compliance; a little history of the approach's development in Western education settings over the last three decades; and how the process unfolds from the invitation to participation and follow-up. For those who have been practicing this way for some time, we hope this will be reassuring; for those new to these concepts, we spell out in some detail so that you might be enticed into appropriate training, knowing a little of what you will be letting yourself in for!

Chapter 8: Shame, Trauma, and Restorative Practice

In this chapter, we draw the links between trauma and shame, or as psychiatrist Paul Conti writes, "Trauma doesn't operate by itself... trauma gets a lot of help from a number of accomplices, chief amongst them is shame" (Conti 2021, p.29). We explore shame's biological and physiological nature as a social alarm—an indicator of a rupture in a relationship when harm is done and we feel let down by others or ourselves. We examine how culture plays a role in what we find shameful in ourselves and others and how shame is used in social regulation—keeping us contained within the norms of acceptable behavior and developing a strong sense of community and connection. This knowledge will help the thinking around the types of interactions with our students and colleagues beyond the school gates. Like trauma, shame (often caused by trauma) has a way of showing up in our own and others' behavior, and it can liberate us from being too quick to draw conclusions about the flaws in someone's character. We can also review school policy and procedures through the lens of shame and help us understand why taking a restorative rather than retributive approach to problem-solving suits the way our brains are designed to work.

Chapter 9: Becoming a Trauma-Informed Restorative Educator: Pulling it All Together

Our final chapter provides a reflection on what we have learned. We offer readers a short inventory which we hope you will use to deepen the conversation about moving our practices and approaches away from outdated philosophies that are potentially trauma-inducing to more brain-science-backed approaches that focus on nervous system regulation. It is a reminder and a call to action that this work needs to be intentional. This chapter also reminds us that our journey is ours, and we need to be accountable for our learning and the continuation of our road.

HOW OUR CHAPTERS ARE ORGANIZED

As we end most chapters or key sections (within chapters), we offer you an opportunity to reflect and commit to changing your thinking and actions. We believe that doing this has value, although we don't know whether or not you will use it. What we do know, however, is that there is a huge difference between the learning that comes from reading and the learning that comes from doing. Please consolidate what you read here and translate it into action. Including the book in an ongoing professional learning community (or even staffroom) book club is worth considering. In this respect, the perspectives of others are vital to our learning and will motivate us to persist with the reading and the conversations that will help create a culture of knowledge and best practice.

We know there will be more to know by the time this book gets to print. Even when our book was a twinkle in our eyes, it has been challenging to keep up, so we ask you to commit to keep learning. We realize that there are different models and explanations of how the brain is structured and how it works. We have settled on a simpler, less complicated version of a model to make sense for ourselves and, we hope, for you, the educator.

If you are reading this book, then we hope you are interested in doing things differently, especially around the issues of your relationships with children and young people and their families, how you connect with them, and how you respond to the times when they are failing to meet your expectations.

We hope it triggers your interest and enjoyment and either challenges your thinking and habits or reassures you that you are on this journey and it's a good one!

This book is a call to action.

CHAPTER 2

A Starting Point: Some Theory, Concepts, and Definitions

Approaches to managing human behaviour are generally grounded in theories (beliefs and understandings about how humans behave, why they behave, and ways to manipulate, change, encourage, and discourage behaviour). These theories often draw from the behavioural sciences, such as psychology and sociology. The challenge for trauma aware education is that the bulk of the more common approaches to "behaviour management" in schools is mostly informed by Behaviourism and is not informed enough by neuroscience.

(DR. JUDITH HOWARD 2022, P.89)

We start this chapter by discussing some basic theoretical underpinnings that guide our approaches to changing the behaviors of our students that are reflected in policy, structures, and practices in our schools. The strategies we typically use, hoping to change the behavior of our students, are based on various theories. Still, we generally have no idea where these ideas were developed—we do what we do because it's always been done that way. An approach that has been adopted enthusiastically by many schools in the West under the "behavior management" umbrella is variously referred to as PBIS, PBL, or PB4L.[1] One theory that underpins this approach is

---

[1] Positive Behavior Intervention and Supports, also known as Positive Behavior for Learning, or Positive Behavior 4 Learning, is a tiered approach to prevention and responses to encourage more positive student behavior.

behaviorism. We examine behaviorism in light of recent research and another theory, self-determination theory. We explore the differences between the theories to appreciate how each might play a role in developing extrinsic and intrinsic motivation. Then, we relate this thinking to how we might create more effective policies and practices around behavior in our schools. We provide a basic outline of restorative and trauma-informed practice and how this might influence our thinking around behavior change. These practices will be explored in more detail in subsequent chapters.

BEHAVIORISM

Behaviorism itself is grounded in theories about behavior modification, developed last century, and most educators can remember that in our training, we heard of B.F. Skinner and his work in the mid-1950s around learning theory. His theory details two ways in which behavior can be modified—by using *classical* and *operant* conditioning. Classical conditioning is a subconscious, automatic, or involuntary response to a stimulus. Operant conditioning (sometimes called instrumental conditioning) is a conscious or voluntary response followed by a consequence such as a reward.

Classical conditioning is best understood with the well-known example of Russian physiologist Ivan Pavlov's experiment with dogs while studying the physiology of digestion. He observed that dogs produced saliva when presented with meat. He discovered that by pairing the ringing of a bell *at the same time* as the meat was presented, the dog eventually salivated when the bell rang, even before the meat arrived. Tapping into our memory to visualize some of our favorite foods, our mouths can fill with saliva—that is *classical* conditioning and an example of our brain's capacity to predict!

Operant conditioning is a concept in psychology that explains how people and animals develop learned responses through the repetition of positive reinforcement (e.g., rewards such as praise, stickers, free time), negative reinforcement (e.g., removal of something unpleasant such as no homework if the task is completed by the end of the lesson), and punishment (e.g., detention for not doing homework).

Operant conditioning is the *reinforcement* of a behavior with a response that comes *after* the behavior: "Do this, and you will get that." There is an assumption that this behavior will likely be repeated because of the reward. The reward is a reinforcement contingent on the "right" behavior. In a school, this would be given by the *adult* (at home, the parent). When we see an inappropriate behavior, we apply a retributive sanction to act as a deterrence (and others watching will also get the message) so that the incidents of this behavior will slowly diminish to the point of eventual extinction. Skinner believed (this is a significant aspect of the theory) that all behavior was a learned response to such changes in the environment; that behavior was only ever about what we want to gain and what we want to avoid.

Operant conditioning assumes that behavior is a matter of motivation, and motivation will increase or decrease depending on the type of reinforcement or sanction. We know how well that works when the same students turn up in detentions over and over again for doing the same things; the same students are suspended from school for repeating the same offenses. When considering this repeated behavior, we often think, "He *knows* how to behave—we have had this conversation many times, so clearly he is *choosing* to behave this way." We follow these ideas and practices often without conscious thought, not realizing how deeply they have been embedded in our neural pathways and habits of thinking. When these strategies don't work, many of us are inclined to blame the child and the family, not policy, practice, environment, or theory.

Alfie Kohn, educator, blogger, and author, argues in his book *Punished by Rewards: The Trouble with Gold Stars, Incentive Plans, A's, Praise, and Other Bribes* (1999, 2018, first published 1993) that these ideas, especially around operant conditioning, have been so widely shared that *they are no longer even noticed* and certainly not challenged enough. We have been firmly socialized into believing this approach is effective, and it seems that it has held us hostage for many years—reflected in our thinking and built into school policy and practice. In this same book, Kohn also reflects that using rewards and punishments sometimes works in the short term, even while it is an example of power over (i.e., command and control) to maintain compliance—and its popularity can be explained simply because rewards and punishments are easy to administer.

Bruce Perry, neuroscientist, child psychiatrist, and early pioneer of the study of childhood trauma, says in his YouTube series *Stress, Trauma, and the Brain: Insights for Educators* (Perry 2020) that if children *already have the skills required*, rewards may work as a reinforcement *in the short term* for some students. Kohn suggests the effectiveness of these rewards (he calls them bribes) wears off over time, so they lose their power to manipulate behaviors, and we find ourselves having to increase the reward/punishment to get the same degree of compliance.

Dr. Lori Desautels and Michael McKnight write in their book *Eyes Are Never Quiet: Listening Beneath the Behaviors of Our Most Troubled Students* (2019) that these traditional approaches work best for the students who need them the least and are much less effective for those we think need them the most! Desautels writes in her book *Intentional Neuroplasticity: Moving Our Nervous Systems and Educational System Toward Post-Traumatic Growth* (2023, p.28):

> Many individuals in the western part of the world have been conditioned, parented, and schooled through a lens of behaviorism. Conventionally, our school systems and structures have embedded behaviorism along with contingency programs that address and focus on compliance and control. Many of these contingency behavioral regulations and handbooks mirror zero tolerance policies from the 1990s and early 2000s, often designed by racially privileged school leaders and groups who have both unintentionally and intentionally increased racial inequities and disparities for our children and youth of color, students from other cultures, and special education populations.

We are so socialized to use rewards and punishments that we rarely stop to consider the risks involved in this approach, especially when our schools have embraced the common three-tiered approach to behavior management (PBIS, PBL, PB4L), popular in many parts of the Western world. There are similar programs that employ behaviorist approaches, so we hope you can interrogate any program your school may be using in light of this section. Remember, if we seek culture change in our schools, these "programs," by their very nature, cannot fully deliver the deep DNA mutations we hope will change mindset and skills. What does need to happen for this to occur is explained later in Chapter 3.

The problem with these reinforcement strategies is that they do not work for all students. Dr. Judith Howard, the author of *Trauma-Aware Education: Essential Information and Guidance for Educators, Education Sites and Education Systems* (2022, p.90), writes that these more common strategies are not informed enough by neuroscience:

> Students living with the outcomes of complex trauma, who already struggle with feeling safe, with relationships, and with emotional regulation, may indeed struggle with negotiating positive reinforcers, negative reinforcers, punishments, and the withholding of rewards, in a manner that results in desired behaviour change.

Dr. Howard also comments that for our most challenging students with complex trauma backgrounds, the social reinforcements in whole-class rewards can be shaming and humiliating, and run the risk of peer condemnation and social exclusion if the student fails to reach the class goal. Their brain, wired for protection rather than connection, fails to respond to the reinforcement schedule that works for most.

In a scathing analysis of PBIS and its claims of being trauma-informed, educators and authors Rhiannon Kim and Alex Venet (2023) comment that its use and the commitment to behaviorism in some 27,000 US schools is so widespread that it prevents some educators from openly questioning the large-scale investment. We are also aware that many schools in Australia and New Zealand also take advantage of the financial support provided by education departments for PBIS implementation without challenging the basic premise and theory of behaviorism. Indeed, Kim and Venet suggest that PBIS is inherently trauma-inducing for a significant proportion of Black, Indigenous, People of Color (BIPOC), neurodivergent, disabled, and disadvantaged students, and those already traumatized.

Behaviorism has additional issues of adding inequity to systems of education already mired in inequity. Venet (2021) points out on her blog *Unconditional Learning* in a post about PBIS:

> In the view of behaviorists, people have no internal motivation or self-determination. To change other people's behavior, you simply reward what you like and punish what you don't like. Building on

this philosophy, PBIS provides "positive supports" for "appropriate" or desired behavior—rewarding what we like, in other words. Based on their (lack of) compliance to behavior expectations, students can be identified for additional interventions meant to change their behavior. But the concepts of "behavior," "appropriate," and "inappropriate" are not neutral. They are political, often rooted in ableism, and often centered in whiteness.

When deciding what is or is not socially acceptable, our implicit biases can often color our view and, in turn, our actions when cultivating discipline in children.

If we take a moment to consider the limitations of the (over) use of this carrot-and-stick approach, Kohn (2018) says that there are hidden costs involved in relying on rewards to reinforce correct behavior. Rewards can:

- *punish:* they are every bit as controlling since it is the adult who has the power and who decides; those who do not rate enough to get the reward (despite their best efforts) are denied the reward, and the effect of this is indistinguishable from punishment

- *rupture and warp relationships:* they do not promote collaboration or a sense of community, but rather competition (issues around fair treatment, playing favorites), and only one student or one team gets the prize

- *ignore reasons:* they demand little from the adult as they are quick fixes. Bribes and threats do not make us look below the surface

- *discourage risk-taking:* if the task is to be rewarded, our focus narrows to do only what is required to complete the task rather than opening up to notice and *"play with possibilities"* (p.63)

- *change how we feel about what we do:* rewards eat away at intrinsic motivation, with extrinsic incentives reducing genuine enthusiasm for the task: "Do this to get that" seems to reduce the interest in doing "this."

Daniel Pink suggests in his book *Drive: The Surprising Truth About What Motivates Us* (2009, p.59) that rewards mindlessly applied and without understanding the *evidence* about what *really* works and what does not may encourage many people to work toward what triggers the reward and no further. This leads to what he refers to as the "Seven reasons carrots and sticks (often) don't work" or "The seven deadly flaws" (Pink 2009, p.59). They can:

- extinguish intrinsic motivation

- diminish performance

- crush creativity

- crowd out good behavior

- encourage cheating, shortcuts, and unethical behavior

- become addictive

- foster short-term thinking.

Pink also suggests that some types of rewards *can* work, if applied delicately. He advises that "any extrinsic reward should be *unexpected* and *only* after the task is complete," referring to it as a "*now that*" reward (p.66). A classroom example might be "Now that you have all worked so hard to complete this unit of work, how about a pizza lunch on Friday?" Acknowledgment and positive feedback and information are more likely to increase intrinsic motivation; for example, "The colors you have used in the map have been very helpful to show the variety of tracks. How do you feel about this map? What do you like about it? What bits did you enjoy doing? Which bits were hard?"

At the 2023 Annual Meeting of the American Medical Association, the House of Delegates received a proposal to remove the American Medical Association's support for applied behavior analysis (ABA) from the Medical Student Section of this professional membership body (American Medical Association 2023). In a bold move, up-and-coming doctors, concerned about the numerous risks and harms of coercive behavioral interventions, proposed Resolution 706, which would have withdrawn the organization's support for ABA, a form of behaviorism most widely used across the globe. While the resolution as proposed was not adopted as written, the resolution pointed to evidence showing the ineffectiveness of the practices and their connections to post-traumatic stress disorder. Here are some points from the evidence noted in the text of the resolution:

- "ABA was conceived in 1961 by Dr. Ole Ivar Lovaas to condition neurotypical behaviors in children he viewed as 'incomplete humans.'"

- "A 2018 study found that Adults with autism who have received ABA are more prone to suicide."

- "ABA has been repeatedly linked to Post Traumatic Stress Disorder (PTSD), with 46% of 460 ABA participants meeting the diagnostic threshold for PTSD in an online survey."

- "Adults with autism have been continuously outspoken about the trauma incurred by ABA practices experienced in their childhood."

Note here that functional behavior assessment processes, used widely in schools to support the top tier of PBIS/PBL/PB4L supports, are derived from ABA, which focuses on analyzing the antecedents to a particular behavior of concern and how the resultant behavior might be modified by changing the responses in the environment. In this analysis, there is not enough reference to neuroscience, which takes a different view about how to interpret behavior. This is not a criticism of the great care and heavily resourced, deep training needed to analyze behavior this way, but rather how the behavior is interpreted. An added issue is that many schools have little access to this resource and may resort to harsher punishments to deter difficult behaviors (Howard 2022).

Psychologist and neuroscientist Lisa Feldman Barrett (2023), in her article "That is not how your brain works," makes this comment, "But sometimes, old scientific beliefs persist, and are even vigorously defended, long after we have sufficient evidence to abandon them."

Weaning ourselves off this contingency approach to change behavior in others requires us to think more constructively about the approaches we habitually use, and about what will work more effectively. But first, we will lead with a brief discussion on the differences between extrinsic and intrinsic motivation and which approach works best to develop motivation in a child or young person to change behavior.

INTRINSIC AND EXTRINSIC MOTIVATION

Self-determination theory, first developed by two academics in the 1970s, Dr. Richard Ryan and Dr. Edward Deci, assumes that people (including students) are motivated by conditions that meet the basic needs of autonomy, competence, and relatedness (Ryan & Deci 2020).

* *Autonomy* is about meeting the needs of agency/choice to initiate and own one's actions and is undermined by experiences of being externally controlled.[2]

* *Competence* is about feeling like something has been mastered and knowing one can succeed and grow.

* *Relatedness* concerns a sense of belonging and relationship connectedness.

If these three basic needs are met, motivation is more likely to become intrinsic, the kind of motivation that means a student will engage in activities done for their own sake or their interest and enjoyment (Ryan & Deci 2000), not because there is a reward at the end of the task but because of curiosity and a desire for challenge. In contrast, *extrinsic* motivation refers to reinforcement strategies (such as rewards) and punishments, which are experienced as controlling and non-autonomous—the decisions being made by the adult.

In a radio broadcast on Radio National (Australian Broadcasting Corporation) Australia for the Health Report (Malcolm 2018), Professor Ryan described self-determination theory as a model to cultivate and sustain the motivation that comes from within—our intrinsic motivation, our sense of self, and our value—so that these are the drivers of behavior rather than carrots and sticks. He spoke about the use of rewards and reinforcements—extrinsic motivation—bringing about the lowest-quality (minimum) behavior and

---

2   A sense of helplessness is often named as a common emotional outcome of trauma and is a significant contributor to a sense of shame. This is worth keeping in mind, as children and young people need to have choices so they can decide on an option instead of it being forced on them.

reducing persistence unless the rewards are continued. In the same radio interview, Ryan discussed what should concern us in our classrooms. For students in a teacher's classroom where the strategies for motivation were more controlling and extrinsic, researchers found that they:

- were less able to do their schoolwork

- were less interested

- wanted lower levels of challenge so there was less chance of making mistakes

- did not take the initiative in the classroom

- were more risk-avoidant

- had less confidence in their academic abilities.

The same researchers found that this decay in motivation resulting from a carrot-and-stick approach was evident *within the first five weeks* of the beginning of the school year.

Dr. Justin Coulson (2023), a respected Australian parenting expert, podcaster, and psychologist, discusses Deci and Ryan's self-determination theory from a parenting perspective. He writes about Deci and Ryan's research in his book titled *The Parenting Revolution* (p.92):

> ...scientific discoveries have pointed to how we can best live life, and how best to raise our children. The most significant and foundational insight from these decades of research: we have clear evidence that when basic psychological needs are supported, people do well and want to do better.

Coulson defines the essence of these needs in "parenting" language as:

- *relatedness*—warm, engaged connections and involvement that minimize control and judgment

- *competence*—scaffolding the skill that needs to be developed in a structured way so that the skill is broken down into achievable bits (there is hope and persistence)

- *autonomy*—encouraging engagement in an activity for the

sake of it, not because we want to avoid being punished or get some reward.

This advice sounds as if it was written for educators, too. Coulson summarizes Ryan and Deci's research like this:

> ...humans are intrinsically drawn to challenge and growth. But we are only drawn to it when we feel that we are choosing it (autonomy), it's tied to our relationships with others (relatedness), and we feel we can master it (competence). (p.100)

Dr. Helen Street (2023), Australian psychologist and Positive Schools and Wellbeing consultant, suggests another way to think about motivation—as other-directed or self-directed. In her translation of Ryan and Deci's self-determination theory, she writes that self-directed motivation contributes to:

- prolonged effort

- determination

- engagement

- positive outcomes

- enhanced well-being.

While with other-directed motivation:

- there is less opportunity to experience a sense of autonomy

- the sense of competence is in someone else's hands (we make these decisions)

- there is lower engagement

- there are poorer long-term outcomes

- there is decreased well-being.

She also advises that it helps to move students from other-directed to self-directed if we do more *asking* than telling when it comes to feedback. We need to ask students to reflect on the task:

- What did they like?

- What went well?

- How have they benefited from the learning process?

- How does it connect with their goals?

Effective feedback focuses more on how the student thinks and feels about their progress than how the teacher feels (Street 2023). Our job is to enable students to internalize the value of learning for its own sake, helping them understand and internalize the school values and behaviors so they become part of their sense of self and identity (internalizing other-directed), and, finally, to become self-directed to achieve their goals.

These basic needs have to be met as much *for our growth as educators* as for the growth and development of our students! Not everything we are asked to do is a matter of choice, so the challenge is finding ways to keep ourselves self-directed!

Some of you reading this will have rejected the notion of rewards for "good" behavior for individuals, classes, or even year levels because it does not resonate with your values about developing young people who only do the right thing when they are supervised, or to get the reward, or to avoid punishment. We hope the arguments in this chapter reassure you that you are on the right track!

EFFECTIVE CONSEQUENCES

Our schools, and, more broadly, our communities, *need* rules and standards that create order and predictability and protect our safety, learning, and relationships. No one would argue about the need for road rules, good manners, or laws that keeps us within reasonable bounds of behavior. None of us would argue either that there are consequences of our behavior—good or bad—for ourselves and others.

As our kids were growing up (Marg), the mantra in our home was "There is nothing we do or don't do that doesn't have an impact on *someone else*." That was not the whole argument, of course, but it was more effective than telling them what would happen to *them* if they broke the rules or what rewards they would get if *they* were compliant—or reached a certain standard of results in their assessments. Focusing on warnings about what will happen to *them* turns their thinking inwards instead of outwards—a concern for self (what's in it for me?) rather than a concern for others.

The trouble with contingency approaches, especially with our young people, is that their original foundations were built on notions of behaviorism (behavior modification), a "command and control" approach, using extrinsic (other-directed) motivation strategies. This is reflected in behavior *management* policies where the adults decide who gets rewarded and who deserves a punishment—*we* are the external locus of control—to improve the likelihood of compliance, when the real job is behavior *development* in a wider context of relationship-based education. This is a much longer-term task that we understand better now that we have been blessed with breakthroughs in the neuroscience of behavior. Are we not looking to develop an *internal* locus of control? Surely. Are we being *intrinsically* motivated to do the right thing? Yes. Something like a moral compass, a sense of right and wrong, a conscience to help with decision-making, and being able to regulate impulses to make considered decisions. If you answer yes to these questions, we need a basic understanding of the structures and functions of the human brain, the science of regulation, self-regulation, and co-regulation—neuroscience 101! This is covered in Chapters 3 and 4.

In developing his collaborative and proactive solutions approach, Dr. Ross Greene (2021) argued that it is a lack of skill, rather than a lack of willpower, that results in the failure of a student to meet our expectations. These skills that we expect young people to have around regulating impulses and managing frustration are complex: executive skills (i.e., thinking, planning, decision-making), use and processing of language and communication, emotional regulation (more about that later), cognitive flexibility, and social skills. No wonder rewards and punishments are limited in their capacity to deliver the goods. Greene (2021, p.162) also expands on this skill set by identifying another group of skills that "foster skills on the more positive side of human nature": empathy, appreciating how one's behavior impacts others, conflict competence, being able to see someone else's point of view, and honesty. Who would have thought being honest might be a skill? These five are part of the repertoire of skills we know a restorative approach can develop over time.

Let us take a moment to think about consequences that are more likely to work. In our book *Building a Trauma-Informed Restorative School: Skills and Approaches for Improving Culture and Behavior* (Brummer & Thorsborne 2020), we suggest consequences should:

- work on solving the problems that led to the behavior

- address the harm caused to individuals and the wider community—this is a negotiated agreement between the parties to meet their needs

- be age- and context-appropriate

- be voluntary rather than imposed—an agreement reached to make amends with willingness rather than coercion

- bring healing to those who were harmed and those that harmed.

In addition, we think effective consequences could:

- likely develop intrinsic motivation by meeting autonomy (agency and choice), competence, and relatedness needs

- begin identifying the *underlying problem* rather than only addressing the outward visible (wrong) behaviors. This requires us to be forensic and free of assumptions, biases, and judgments

- begin to *address the issues* contributing to the problem (including system issues)

- focus on working *with* the student instead of *doing to* them

- encourage the development of skills that may be missing from the young person's repertoire—empathy, honesty, conflict competence, realizing the impact of their behavior on others, and seeing another's point of view (Greene 2021)

- give a voice to those *in* the problem in the problem-solving—after all, those who are affected by the problem are the ones who understand it best and could contribute to the solutions

- focus on the harm done to others and the harm to relationships with these others—this is outward-looking and requires looking beyond "Poor me, now I am being punished."

In a keynote at the biannual Trauma Aware Schooling Conference in Brisbane, Australia, in 2022, Dr. Lori Desautels (2022) posed this question:

> What if we thought of consequences as experiences? What experiences does this child need to feel safe and connected so he or she will stay in the classroom, complete assignments, or make curfew? What if we replaced the words behavior management with behavior engagement?

How would the processes and dialogue we use need to change? What if we considered consequences a *process*, not a pre-ordained outcome listed in the policy, built on behavior modification theory? It is clear from the list of what might make consequences more effective that we need to emancipate ourselves from long-held beliefs about traditional approaches to behavior management that are a result of our socialization—the use of detentions, suspensions, exclusions, restraints, corporal punishment. Often these are a kind of knee-jerk reaction that involves a retributive sanction because "It has always been done that way."

A deputy principal in a large urban high school in Australia tells the story of working with the head of the science faculty, who was struggling to give up these ideas about behaviorist consequences. The deputy principal reminded him that we don't treat snakebite these days by sucking the venom out of the bite—a once-common approach. A more effective approach, based on science, is to bind the affected limb and reduce movement so that the venom does not circulate as readily via the lymphatic system. The head of science had to agree that the scientific evidence did recommend another way!

It is also useful to point out that there is such a thing as the research/evidence–practice gap—the time it takes (approximately 17 years) for a new idea to be accepted by the general public or a particular industry, such as healthcare; the apparent disconnect between best practice and actual practice (Munro & Savel 2016). These new ideas are disruptive of current paradigms around behavior change, particularly in education, and are welcomed by some and challenging for others.

Having been a pioneer of restorative approaches to problem-solving since the mid-1990s (Marg), I can attest to the time lag between the idea and its uptake and am deeply grateful that I have stayed around long enough to see a significant increase in interest and appetite for more relational approaches in education.

One final point to make about the mindset around behaviorist approaches is that of accountability. When we raise the notion of consequences with educators and the wider school community, including parents, we ask, "What is the purpose of a consequence?" Answers typically include a wish list like this:

- Long-term behavior change.

- Learning what not to do.

- Deterrence and sending this message to others.

- Becoming more reflective.

- Being held accountable (usually misunderstood to be achieved through punishment).

For many educators and parents, a simple word-association exercise using the word *consequence* or even *justice* reveals a long-held belief that a proper consequence must involve punishment—inflicting some pain and suffering in response to the pain and suffering caused. Anything else is too soft and does not teach compliance. No one is arguing about the need for compliance. We suggest here that compliance can be achieved by taking a different approach to accountability, which develops a strong sense of responsibility, connectedness, and belonging. Punishment cannot deliver on this.

WHAT ABOUT BIAS AND PREJUDICE IN OUR DECISION-MAKING?

We cannot examine the issue of consequences without exploring notions of implicit bias and prejudice and how these have crept into our cultures and influenced the systems and practices we inhabit. We need to understand the impact of bias and prejudice on our behavior and, therefore, our responses to a young person's behavior.

What do these terms mean, and how do they happen? *Implicit* bias can be defined as *internal* beliefs not founded on facts about someone or a particular group of individuals. *Prejudice* is the outward/external manifestation of our biases (our explicit bias). It becomes evident in discriminatory practices such as higher suspension rates and other punishments for students of color and students with diagnosed or undiagnosed diverse needs and mental health issues. It is helpful to consider this from a biological and biographical perspective, which requires knowledge about how our brains work, what we are born with (what is innate), and what is learned. Bias and prejudice are learned.

Paul Holinger, psychoanalyst, psychiatrist, and co-author of *What Babies Say Before They Can Talk: The Nine Signals Infants Use to Express Their Feelings* (Holinger & Doner 2003), helps new parents understand how babies communicate via the affects of enjoyment-joy (laughing and smiling) and distress-anguish (crying). He writes in his articles and blogs about many issues that parents face, including his understanding of how *difference* (the trigger for bias and prejudice) can be explained by biology and biography.

Babies and toddlers are attracted to things and people that are novel and different (the biological component). These are sources of interest and enjoyment, provided the difference is not too great and, therefore, overwhelming—or provided they have not been taught to fear, be disgusted by, or be too distressed by differences by adults in their lives (Holinger 2018). So, while we are born for novelty and connection, experience (our biography) over time can change these patterns of thinking about "others" (Holinger 2022). Much of this becomes embedded in implicit memory in how we see the world and those who inhabit it with us—in the same way, behaviorism has seeped into our thinking and beliefs about responding to non-compliance.

So, what do we do about these patterns of thinking that show bias or prejudice? How do we transform these rejecting/disconnecting thoughts and behaviors into tolerance and interest in differences? What does this require us to do? This asks us to consider the three intersecting journeys we have outlined in our introductory chapter; that is, to reflect on what this means for our personal, professional, and social justice approaches. We must ask ourselves to:

- be aware of and honestly confront our biases and prejudices (and how they show up) and consider these influences that play a part in any decision-making we are party to

- be aware of how these biases and prejudices play out in the discrimination, inequities, and disparities that might emerge in policies, systems, and data that we are immersed in

- stay with the discomfort this awareness might raise, even at the classroom level, and make time to explore the issues causing the discomfort safely

- practice curiosity about "others," however different they may seem

- seek multiple perspectives around an issue.

In a general sense, the answers lie in education and providing a range of experiences that schools are so well placed to provide, such as:

- making social and emotional learning a priority

- using circle pedagogy to build and sustain connections and learn about each other

- teaching young people how to exchange ideas about issues without conflict and ruptures and with respectful language

- having sufficient representation on the staff of "differentness" so our young people can relate to someone like them, celebrating and valuing differences

- leaning *toward* those who are different and seeking them out to learn more about them

- being radically welcoming to everyone who enters our classroom, even when they are late

- modeling inclusion

- being prepared to give space for dialogue around the "-isms" and discrimination[3] that push us apart unless we are vigilant.

This is the perfect point in this chapter to raise the possibility of another approach to problem-solving, to rethink the whole issue of behaviorism and consequences based on the philosophy and principles of restorative justice.

RESTORATIVE PRACTICE

The following is a summary of this philosophical approach to problem-solving. It is covered in more detail in Chapter 7, which discusses restorative approaches.

Restorative practice[4] is an approach to problem-solving built on the philosophy and principles of restorative justice. When we unpack the basics of this approach, we can see that the questions that might be asked after something happens are very different from a retributive mindset that asks: *What happened? What rules have been broken? Who is to blame? What does our policy say about what punishment is deserved?*

In a school setting, the school policy/code of conduct usually sets out a range of inappropriate behavior (from minor to serious) with a menu of options that educators might use. A policy defines who has the power to suspend and exclude (or cane or paddle[5]) and other

---

3   Racism, classism, sexism and gender identity, nationalism, multiculturalism, religious, linguistic, and neurological discrimination.
4   Restorative practice is also known as RJE—restorative justice in education— restorative measures, restorative approaches, even relational approaches.
5   Paddling is a form of corporal punishment that involves striking a student's buttocks with a wooden paddle.

forms of punishment that the classroom teacher can use. In other words, what will happen *to* you if you do these things—or even if you do not do something you should have—and how you will be held accountable. This comes with an expectation that you will "toe the line" and not repeat the behavior that got you into trouble. Rarely are you asked to be accountable directly to the people your behavior has affected.

The restorative mindset poses different questions:

- What happened?

- Who has been harmed?

- What are their needs?

- Whose responsibility is it to meet those needs?

Howard Zehr (1990, 2015) asks us to view misbehavior (and crime) through a different lens—as a violation of people and relationships (think ruptures), which creates obligations and liabilities (who will take responsibility?)—and to consider a way forward that seeks to heal and make things right.

Chris Marshall (n.d.), Emeritus Professor and former Chair of the Diana Unwin Chair of Restorative Justice at Victoria University, Aotearoa, New Zealand, presenting a knowledge seminar [four video series] about restorative justice practices in schools for the Ministry of Justice in New Zealand in 2015, confirms the limited effectiveness of traditional punitive responses and how counterproductive they are in developing a strong sense of belonging that can buffer children and young people against their difficult circumstances and adverse childhood experiences. In other words, justice and discipline remediate rather than retaliate because punishment is not empowered to heal. A better question asks, "What is needed to regain the trust of others?"

Let's reconsider Ross Greene's (2021) work around the "skills that foster the better side of human nature": empathy, appreciation of how one's behavior impacts others, conflict competence, seeing someone else's point of view, and honesty. We can now understand that the simplicity and ease of the quick fix of behaviorist approaches (e.g., rewards and sanctions) do not come anywhere near achieving this growth in student development. Far better to think about behavior *development* and *relational* accountability within the context of relationship-based education.

If a school adopts this philosophy, the consequence for an incident of inappropriate behavior becomes a process that takes a different approach from accountability as it seeks to meet the needs of those affected, including the needs of the responsible person. Over the last three decades, elementary, middle, and high schools have adapted these processes to cope with various situations in classrooms, playgrounds, buildings, staffrooms, and the early years, and for those with special needs. This is referred to as the restorative continuum, and we believe it is essential that members of the school community come to know and understand that this is "the way we do things around here."

There is agency/autonomy in this approach—students and young people participate voluntarily (some, to be sure, reluctantly at first), and we need to be invitational in our approach. Michelle Stowe (2023), Dublin Restorative Practices consultant, has created a list of "restorative sound bites" in a blog connected to her online training, focusing on invitational ways to engage with a young person when problem-solving is needed. One of those restorative sound bites is a relational invitation: *"I'm here to listen to you and I want to understand your perspective. Would you be open to doing that with me too?"*

The rest of the exploratory sequence explores "What happened?" and then the "How come this happened?" so that those involved can better understand the motivation or intention of the behavior. The people affected get to explain the impact of the incident/s with "What has this been like for you? What has been the worst of it?" Chapter 7 has more detail about the restorative process and the sorts of open-ended questions typically used to encourage dialogue.

If the people in the problem can reach a shared understanding of what happened and make sense of the reasons for the behavior and the collective harm caused, the process will likely generate empathy within this group. With luck, there might be an apology[6] or at least an acknowledgment of this harm. This allows those harmed some

---

6   Apology is a complex social skill, and the style of it is very much influenced by our culture. Our advice to adults here is that if you want a genuine, authentic apology from a young person, you had better teach them its purpose and how to do it!

relief and those responsible a sense of not being judged as a bad person. If this sense of relief is reached, then the process is poised to develop a plan focused on making things right and starting the problem-solving process around the contributing factors.

Many of you reading this section will be reassured that your beliefs about the importance of healthy relationships in educating young people have been affirmed. Others may still struggle with beliefs that we as educators should have all the power, that we are always right, that compliance at all costs is essential so chaos is kept at bay, and that if *we* admit to letting others down in some way, it will make us vulnerable and limit our authority. Be reassured that nothing is more powerful to rebuild trust than modeling that we are willing to take responsibility for contributing to a problem.

The next issue for us to consider is what stress does to the behavior of students (and us), how it manifests in what we see in behavior, and how we respond. In choosing the word stress as an introduction to trauma-informed practice, we are encompassing a continuum of stress that, at one end, has capital "T" traumas (Perry & Winfrey 2021) and at the other end, small "t" traumas/stressors that deeply affect the capacity of young people to learn and that play a huge role in what we often assume is non-compliance. It's these assumptions that need to be challenged.

TRAUMA-INFORMED PRACTICE

We should define trauma before considering what trauma-informed practice involves and how it might be integrated with restorative practice. Dr. Paul Conti, in an interview with Andrew Huberman (2022) in the podcast episode *Dr. Paul Conti: Therapy, Treating Trauma & Other Life Challenges*, on the Huberman Lab, provides the following definition:

> Trauma happens when something occurs that overwhelms our coping skills and leaves us different as we move forward...it changes the way our brains function, and then these changes are evident in us as we move forward through life.

When this knowledge is applied in the school setting, we are asked to consider the lives of our learners to know what may have overwhelmed their coping skills and what may have derailed the development of their brains, becoming evident in behavior that we *can* see but often misinterpret.

Acute traumatic events can include:

- weather events like hurricanes, earthquakes, floods, bushfires/wildfires, tsunamis, and prolonged drought

- human-made events such as mass shootings in schools or other urban settings, wars, rape, aggravated robberies, and car accidents.

Chronic trauma can be understood as something that is not a one-off, but rather when a child or young person is subjected to ongoing toxic stress that may be a result of a range of adverse childhood experiences (ACEs) such as:

- neglect and abuse

- household dysfunction, including family violence, drug abuse, mental illness, parental conflict and separation, and incarceration of a caregiver

- poverty (especially intergenerational)

- pandemics (witness the recent and ongoing impacts of Covid-19 on our mental health, physical health, our capacity to earn a living, and deaths)

- disadvantage and discrimination around race, cultural differences, religious beliefs and affiliations, gender, sexual orientation, and disabilities.

On top of these issues that can contribute significantly to changes in brain function, we now better understand the impacts of *intergenerational* trauma on our Indigenous First Nation populations due to colonization, on refugees from war-torn regions in our world, and on those now affected by climate change and displacement.

We also now know that if any of these acute or chronic traumas happen in the early (first 1000 days) or adolescent brain development of the child, many of the symptoms show up as behaviors that look like:

- aggression, violence, yelling, verbal abuse (fight)

- avoidance, procrastination, running away, school refusal (flight)

- unresponsiveness, zoning out, daydreaming (freeze).

In a behaviorist context, these behaviors amount to non-compliance and, therefore, "deserve" a punitive response to reduce the likelihood of more of the same. But this and other environmental responses, such as rewards and negative reinforcement, will not assist in addressing the impact of these experiences on brain development. With a trauma-informed practice lens, these behaviors can be considered evidence of the *dysregulation* of the nervous system, and a result of the impact of stressors on brain development (more about this in Chapters 3, 4, and 6). The question must then be asked: "What can we not see?" And what can we do (without being therapists) to help develop behaviors that improve connection and engagement in learning, address the present behaviors, and develop a future orientation?

In their book *The Boy Who Was Raised as a Dog: And Other Stories from a Child Psychiatrist's Notebook*, Perry and Szalavitz (2006) are optimistic that schools present a unique opportunity to create a safe, caring environment to make a real difference because students are at school six hours a day. Their advice includes the need to:

- build and rebuild trust between adults and children

- create patterned rhythmic and repetitive experience with a trusted adult to change the child's brain

- redevelop the brain from the bottom up (safety first)

- practice patience, repetition, and reinforcement.

Two questions that might guide our thinking are: "What can the child's history and behavior tell us about what has happened to them?" and "What do they need to experience and learn through our relationship with them?" (Kelly 2017), especially since the behaviors they exhibit may make it very challenging for us (the adults) to achieve these outcomes. We must understand ourselves well enough to know the triggers that cause us distress and be prepared to work on becoming that calm, trusted adult, however long it takes to build that trust.

It might look as if we are simply now making excuses for wayward (trauma) behavior and feeling sorry for the child who has been through tough times. It may look as if we have become permissive around holding them accountable and that they "get away with stuff." When we integrate restorative approaches to achieve genuine accountability and seek to understand, we *are* deeply interested in the triggers for the young person who "did the thing," their story, their dysregulation, and their lack of skill. We cannot do that unless we have a sense of the load they may be carrying in their backpack.

Trauma-informed practice is *not* about making excuses. It is about understanding and then knowing how to respond in effective ways.

At this point, we hope that we have convinced you of the need to move away from behavioristic approaches toward more relational approaches built into restorative practice: to be prepared to look under the mat of the presenting behavior with curiosity and calmness.

Returning to the point that we made early in this chapter, we encourage you to consider that genuine trauma-informed approaches can have much more successful outcomes when we give up on notions of viewing behavior through a compliance/noncompliance lens. It is better to use restorative thinking and processes for problem-solving. Or the reverse, when our restorative approaches are informed by an understanding of the adverse experiences that have shaped our students' brains, we will do much better with our well-informed practices.

CENTRAL IDEAS

★ Contingency approaches (use of rewards and sanctions) to behavior development (behaviorism) are limited in their effectiveness in developing skills that do not yet exist and, for those students with a background of complex trauma and adverse childhood experiences, can cause more harm.

★ Motivation (to change behavior and persist with learning) can be extrinsic (other-directed, based on contingency strategies) or intrinsic (self-directed, based on creating the conditions for autonomy, competence, and relatedness). Strategies that develop intrinsic motivation are more effective as we seek to change behavior. Overuse of contingency approaches has been shown to decrease motivation.

★ Many school behavior policies are built around behaviorism theory. These approaches do not recognize or consider the impact of trauma on brain development. Implementing restorative, trauma-informed approaches requires that schools rethink policy and practice based on the latest research in neuroscience.

★ Implicit biases or prejudices can show up in our decision-making around consequences when using contingency approaches.

★ Contingency approaches are limited in their effectiveness in developing such skills as empathy, appreciation of how one's behavior impacts others, conflict competence, seeing someone else's point of view, and honesty. Punitive approaches are limited in their capacity to heal the harm that an incident has caused.

★ Restorative and trauma-informed approaches to consequences take a much broader view of underlying problems causing a problem.

★ Restorative and trauma-informed approaches take a relational approach to problem-solving, built around prevention, regulation and co-regulation, relationship building, maintenance, and repair. This is informed by the latest neuroscience research aimed at developing a strong sense of connection and belonging, essential for prosocial behavior development.

REFLECTION QUESTIONS

✓ How aware are you of how influenced you are/have been by theories on how best to affect and change behavior and the use of contingency approaches?

✓ When thinking about other-directed and self-directed theories of motivation, which of these have helped you persist when the going gets tough?

✓ To what extent have you kept yourself up-to-date about the latest research on the neuroscience of behavior and behavior change? Have you been able to apply this knowledge to understand how student behavior might result from past harms and how this shapes brain development?

✓ Do you have a good sense of what makes a consequence effective besides reducing the likelihood of the challenging behavior persisting and improving compliance?

✓ When considering the impact of policies and practices in your school, is the data showing evidence of bias and prejudice, and are you willing to challenge this?

✓ Are you working deliberately to create a strong sense of inclusion and belonging so that your classroom welcomes all, leaning towards those who are different and encouraging respectful dialogue to build social capital and a safe space?

The next chapter is an introduction to the neuroscience of brain and behavior development, and in enough detail, we hope, for your understanding of the structure and function of key parts of the brain. We believe this information is critical to understand behavior through a different lens.

CHAPTER 3

The Neuroscience of Behavior

In Chapter 2, we described behaviorism and its limited capacity to explain behavior other than a cynical view that children behave to "get things" or "get out of things." To become trauma-informed and restorative is to rethink the root causes of human behavior. This is especially true as a child's and adolescent's brain undergoes amazing development during its formative years. Sadly, much of the current restorative work being done in schools across the globe is steeped in this outdated behavioristic view of behavior, which is more about improving the likelihood of compliance rather than working *with* the student's brain. Current neuroscience has cast credible doubt on the plausibility of behaviorism, if not completely turning it on its head.

Our brains use more energy than any other organ in the human body, and to conserve energy, the brain infers and hypothesizes to anticipate and predict what to do in a given situation. This means that external stimuli and interoceptive information are processed through past experiences to predict what happens in our world. When we learn more about the brain's capacity to predict, could it be that the behaviors we see in others are simply the result of their brain predicting how to cope with the world around them? Might it be that behavior is less intentional? Children interact with their environment, and when they are not behaving as expected, perhaps we might consider aspects of the environment that might need changing rather than laying the total responsibility for change with the child.

In this chapter, as we explain how the human brain develops and functions, it will be much clearer to understand that behaviorism is not just outdated, it is a dark view of children and adolescents that paints them as intentionally naughty, malicious, and manipulative. We will provide some simple explanations of the complexities of implicit and explicit memory, which works to help predict our responses, and how the development, structure, and function of the different parts of the brain support our view that we have to change our minds about behavior and compliance/non-compliance.

CONCEPTUAL MODEL OF THE BRAIN

There are dozens of models of the brain. The brain is represented in various ways depending on the neuroscientist, trainer, author, or speaker. Some describe it as bottom to top, top to bottom, while others divide the brain into sections or layers and others by regions and functions.[1] Most models, if not all, oversimplify the complexity of the brain so we can summarize and conceptualize how it evolved, develops over the lifespan, and functions at the moment. This model-making is needed for us to teach and talk about the brain in ways that make sense (Barrett 2017).

American neuroscientist and psychiatrist Dr. Bruce Perry created a model that helps simplify this complexity and understand the brain's architecture, evolution, and functioning. His model, the Neurosequential Model of Therapeutics (Perry 2006; see also Perry and Winfrey 2021, pp.23–28), was first developed to explain to patients in therapeutic settings how their brains work and what may have caused their brains to adapt differently from other people in light of trauma, stress, and other developmental risk factors. Further development of this model has been designed to explain brain function in various professional settings; hence, Perry's latest iteration for educators is the Neurosequential Model in Education (Neurosequential Network, n.d.).

Perry's Neurosequential Model (Perry 2006) outlines some basics about the structure and functioning of the brain. We have tried to summarize and paraphrase below:

---

1   Disclaimer: There are many different models and explanations of how the brain is structured and how it works. We have settled on a simpler, less complicated model to make sense for ourselves and, we hope, for you, the educator.

- Our brains have roughly 86 billion neurons.

- The brain is undeveloped at birth and continues to grow and adapt to changes through life experiences. This process is called neuroplasticity.

- The brain evolves, develops, and functions from the bottom up and from the inside out, and processes information sequentially, reflecting this developmental structure.

- All layers and systems in the brain can hold various forms of memory and can respond/react to the world through a system of predictive anticipation of what will happen next based on what has happened in the past. We process the present moment through the stored information our brain already has from the experiences that have already happened to us.

- The brain assesses all incoming information from the outside world through our five senses (i.e., exteroception) and our inner world (i.e., interoception) as positive, negative, or neutral based on previously stored memories or past experiences and relationships.

- The "state" of our nervous system is contagious. As warm-blooded, hairy mammals, we are social animals. Herd-like connections to each other's emotional states provide us with an additional layer of safety. When we sense danger collectively, alerting each other unconsciously, we can activate our awareness of danger. This is often referred to as "flocking."

The following four-layer graphic, the Neurosequential Model (NM) Brain Heuristic (Figure 3.1), familiar to many who have read Perry's work, represents the organization and architecture of the brain along with its core regulatory networks. It has four main layers representing the brain systems that are integrated and connected: the brainstem, the diencephalon, the limbic system, and the cortex. As we will describe next, each system is responsible for different functions, each holding various types of memory and each able to motivate behavior in response to various stimuli.

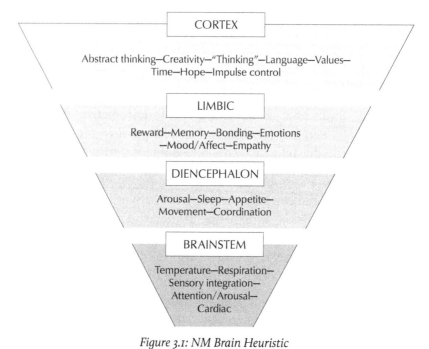

Figure 3.1: NM Brain Heuristic

Brainstem

Our brainstem is the oldest in evolutionary terms and forms the bottom layer of the brain. It is the most basic structure of the brain and is fully developed at birth, meaning that when a baby is born, this part of the brain is already online. While the brainstem may be perceived as the least complex of all the layers, it is the layer that processes all our sensory information, both interoceptive and exteroceptive. It holds the memories of and controls primarily regulatory, vital life functions, such as body temperature, blood pressure, breathing, consciousness, heart rate, sleep, swallowing, and excretion—essential functions we are born with—and is essential to keeping these processes running smoothly without conscious effort throughout our lives.

The brainstem also can interact with the limbic area of the brain (see "Limbic system") to create reactive emotional states like anger or fear—the layer of the brain where our threat response systems of fight, flight, freeze, faint, flock, and feign get triggered when a threat is detected. In such times, the brainstem is truly the "boss." It is always on guard, searching for safety or danger cues from this sensory information to mediate states of arousal and alertness. Because the lower brain structures are necessary for survival, they tend to be somewhat rigid and compulsive. Sometimes, the brainstem is referred to as the reptilian or guard-dog/wild brain in younger children.

Diencephalon

The next layer is the diencephalon (e.g., the motor brain, sometimes called the midbrain). It forms a bridge between the brainstem and higher regions of the brain. It is fully developed between the ages of four and six years old. It processes and coordinates movement, including fine and gross motor functions and facial expressions. Together with the cerebellum, it is important for balance. This part of the brain also holds the memories of movement; we would call this "muscle memory," such as our memory of how to walk, talk, dance, play an instrument, or even hold still. We can repeat these actions because this part of our brain remembers how.

Limbic system

The limbic system is our "social-emotional" brain. Lying above the diencephalon and below the cerebral cortex, it links the conscious, intellectual functions of the cerebral cortex (i.e., the top part of the brain, discussed next) with the unconscious, autonomic functions of the lower brain structures. Development of the limbic system begins once the infant is born, is fully developed between the ages of 11 and 12, and is shaped in response to genetic makeup, temperament, and experience.

Two important brain structures of the limbic system are the hippocampus and amygdala. Together, they use memories and information about how our body works and current sensory input to generate emotional responses to situations, influencing how we respond to the world around us. The hippocampus is essential in forming memories and acts as a "memory indexer" that sends memories to the appropriate part of the brain for long-term storage and retrieves them when needed. We depend on the amygdala to warn of impending danger, activate the body's stress response, and regulate emotions such as anxiety, aggression, fear conditioning, emotional memory, and social cognition.

Our limbic system is critical to our survival. It monitors danger and judges unpleasant and pleasant experiences for survival purposes, and what follows are the resulting emotions or what we call affect (Barrett 2017). If it detects danger or opportunity, these areas react, sending signals that elicit visceral sensations, such as triggering a stress response, preparing the body for fight or flight (Roozendaal, McEwen, & Chatterjee 2009). Even the most subtle feelings can greatly affect our decisions, such as choosing what and when to eat, where and when we sleep, our sleep quality, and whom we befriend and detest. Long-term stress in the amygdala can have long-term consequences, such as anxiety and cognitive performance, in association with other areas in the brain.

The limbic system is the brain's response center "for coping with the challenges of living within our complex social networks" (van der Kolk 2014, p.56). Our limbic system is acutely sensitive to the emotional states of others; we all know how contagious someone's anger, distress, fear, shame, or joy can be. Moreover, our earliest life experiences contribute to our emotional and perceptual map of the world. If a child feels safe and loved, the brain becomes specialized in exploration, play, and cooperation; if frightened and unwanted, it specializes in managing feelings of fear and abandonment. These early life experiences shape the limbic structures devoted to emotions and memory, but later experiences can significantly modify these structures for better or worse. While the limbic system may be fully developed by the pre-teen years, the cortex, which helps to regulate it, does not mature for another decade or more. This means that our teens and adolescents are working with emotional systems that have a greater impact on decision-making than their higher cortical control systems. That is, their emotional brains are stronger than their rational thinking brains. They may blurt stuff out they did not mean, laugh at inappropriate times, feel disappointed and hurt more intensely than at any other time, and make decisions in the company of others that they would not if they were by themselves.

Cortex

The cerebral cortex sits at the top of the brain and is responsible for our highest mental processing and consciousness. It is divided into the neocortex, responsible for abstract thinking, reflecting, and higher reasoning, and the prefrontal cortex, responsible for concrete thinking, such as judgment, and is important in retrieving our autobiographical stories. Both areas are important for a wide range of cognitive functions, and they work together to help us process and interpret the world around us. Our cortex makes us uniquely human; it allows us to process language and plan our time, be aware of the past, present, and future, and hold our values and beliefs. It is the last part of the brain to develop fully, with maturation extending well into the mid-to-late twenties and early thirties.

By the age of five, the core regulatory networks of the brain are set up. By the time a child is six, their brain has reached about 90 to 95 percent of its adult physical size.

While the early years are important for brain development, brain plasticity and remodeling happen extensively during adolescence. Brain neuroplasticity refers to the brain's capacity for neural circuits—connections and pathways for thought, emotion, and movement—to change or reorganize in response to genomic and environmental cues (Horvath 2023). These structural and functionally important changes are necessary for survival and reproduction and play a critical role during childhood and adolescence in shaping cognitive and behavioral developmental processes (Fandakova & Hartley 2020). The offset in time regarding the development of the adolescent's brain sets up a mismatch between the fully developed limbic system and the underdevelopment of the cortex, specifically the pre-frontal cortex, which controls impulses. On the one hand, teens are more prone to poorer judgment; on the other hand, this stage of brain development allows them to adapt readily to their environment to make enormous strides in thinking and socialization (Giedd 2016).

HOW THE BRAIN PROCESSES INFORMATION

Our brain uses two major sources of information to keep us safe, alive, and functioning. The first is from the outside world, using information from our five senses: visual, auditory, tactile (touch), olfactory (smell), and taste. The second source is from our inside world (somatic or interoception—what is happening in our body), such as thirst, hunger, energy levels, breathing, our need to use the bathroom, or the location of the pain.

No information goes directly to any higher part of the brain before being processed in the lower systems first (refer to Figure 3.1: NM Brain Heuristic). Incoming data is first processed in the brainstem, then in the motor brain (diencephalon), before reaching the limbic system, and finally the cortex, provided no threat is detected (real or perceived). Dr. Bruce Perry (Perry & Winfrey 2021) explains it this way:

> All experience is processed from the bottom up, meaning, to get to the top, "smart" part of our brain, we have to go through the lower, not-so-smart part. This sequential processing means that the most primitive, reactive part of our brain is the first part to interpret and act on the information coming in from our senses. Bottomline: *Our brain is organized to act and feel before we think.* This is also how our brain develops—sequentially, from the bottom up. The developing infant *acts* and *feels*, and these actions and feelings help organize how they will begin to *think.* (p.29)

MEMORY AND THE PREDICTIVE BRAIN

Memory is the ability to store and retrieve information when needed. Dr. Bruce Perry explains memory by saying: "Memory is the capacity to carry forward in time some element of an experience," and continues, "memory is what the brain does, how it composes us and allows our past to help determine our future. In no small part memory makes us who we are..." (Perry & Szalavitz 2006, p.27).

Memory is explicitly tied to our identity. Our nervous systems are unique to each of us, built on memory from layers of previous and current experiences. With only past experiences as a guide, our brains use stored experience in our memory to make meaning of the present and anticipate how to handle future experiences, meaning we process and experience the present world through the lens of every experience our brains have stored to determine what is safe or a potential threat to our well-being. This helps us understand how two people can experience the same event yet respond differently. Each person's prediction of what will happen is based on what has already happened to them. We also learn from each new experience, allowing us to adapt to an ever-changing world constantly. This brain adaptability is neuroplasticity, the term given to the process by which neural circuits in our brain develop and are modified by experience and learning. Neuroplasticity helps us to build memory.

Explained next is explicit and implicit memory (i.e., two types of long-term memory). Each plays an important role in our ability to process our current experiences.

Implicit memory

Implicit memory is present at birth and begins to develop in utero. It informs how we think and behave. Our implicit memory does "not require conscious, focal attention," it includes our "perceptions, emotions, bodily sensations, and behavioral response patterns," and "in its unintegrated form does not convey a sense that something is being recalled from the past" (Seigel 2020, p.505). It comes in many forms and is essential for most biological functioning, including muscle memory, immune system memory, emotional memory, and cellular memory. Gabor Maté, in Chapter 10 of his book *The Myth of Normal*, titled "Trouble at the Threshold: Before We Come Into the World," cites studies that indicate that "the developmental origin of adult disease begins in the womb" (Maté & Maté 2022, p.142), showing that before birth and after, a fetus or young child is "particularly vulnerable to the environment," which sets the stage for many behavioral and physical health challenges.

Implicit memories are unconscious and automatic; we do not have a conscious sensation that we recall something without thinking about it, such as how to perform tasks we do every day or our ability to perform them. These are habits formed through repetition until we reach unconscious competence, such as playing a musical instrument, riding a bike, or navigating a familiar place in your home at night without turning on the lights. Other experiences include recognizing colors or familiar faces and scents. Implicit memories are recalled from the past yet feel as if they are in the present; you recognize the scent of freshly baked cookies that reminds you of your grandmother's baking when you were a child. Implicit memories are also based on associations. If a child experiences fear while in a red room, it is more likely that they will experience fear again when put in another red room. If past experiences of the smell of alcohol on an adult's breath are associated with violence, this smell may trigger fear. Implicit memory is how we store implicit bias and build stereotypes of others.

My (Marg) own half-sister, Billie, to whom this book is dedicated, began life already challenged. Her mother, dying of tuberculosis while pregnant, died ten days after giving birth to her. I cannot imagine the sadness, grief, and stress that were part of her intrauterine experience. She was cared for by her maternal grandmother until my dad met my mother a couple of years later, and a new family came along—a stepmother and two new siblings. Her subsequent struggles with depression, inflammatory disease, and prescription medication addictions make so much sense to me now. I wish I had known about this while I was growing up. I suspect I would have been a better sister.

Explicit memory

Explicit memory is our recallable memory of the narrative that is our lives. It begins developing between 18 months and three years of age, depending on which model of the brain is studied. Dan Siegel (2020, p.505) defines explicit memory as "the layer of memory that during recall is coupled with an internal sensation of remembering. There are two forms: semantic memory (factual) and episodic memory (with repeated episodes being called "autobiographical)." Explicit memory, indexed in the hippocampus in the limbic system part of the brain, is what we rely on for recall—the supermarket shopping list we left behind (factual) and the stories we tell (both episodic and autobiographical). We access this kind of memory when, in restorative processes, we ask, "What happened?" "What were you thinking when that happened?" and, "What have you thought about since?"

Stress and memory

It is important to note here that stress can impact memory. Dan Siegel (2020) writes, "stressful experiences may take the form of highly emotional events or, when the stress is overwhelming, overtly traumatizing experiences" (p.150). In describing the impact of trauma on memory, the Centre for YouthAOD Practice Development (n.d.) produced *The Out of Home Care Toolbox*. This lists several challenges for children experiencing trauma, such as the inability to form narrative memory or "to make sense of their experience or build narrative about their life that draws meaning and understanding." What this means then, from a restorative and behavior perspective, is that there will be difficulties for the student in:

- making sense of what happened in an incident

- remembering the details of the event/incident—this becomes an issue when we ask, "What happened? Where were you? Who was with you? What happened next?"

- managing more cognitive tasks in the classroom that involve learning, remembering, and problem-solving.

Again, we contend that understanding the basics of what happens in the brain is critical knowledge for us as educators as we seek better ways to help young people navigate through the complexities of life in the classroom, corridors, and playgrounds. It also enables us to move away from theories around behaviorism.

Prediction error

What happens when our predictive capabilities go awry, as sometimes happens? Lisa Feldman Barrett says that "through prediction and correction, [our] brain continually creates and revises [our] mental model of the world" (Barrett 2017, p.62). Our brain is a simulating machine that makes predictions based on stored knowledge, but sometimes these predictions are incorrect. Barrett calls this a prediction error. Being human is to error; this is how we learn. As Barrett explains, as adults, our "predictions [are not] too far off base" (p.62). We can have a mishap in judgment and behavior but usually we self-correct; our brain changes the prediction. For example, you walk past a garden hose, mistakenly thinking it is a snake, or you misjudge the depth of a curb and trip as you cross the street. If we have a history of trauma, the adversity is likely the information we use to make predictions; therefore, our predictions can be skewed. For example, we fail to see red flags where they are present or to see them when they are not. We misinterpret other people's actions or words because the lens we see them through anticipates that what comes next will be negative.

As we review in this chapter, the child and adolescent brains are a work in progress, developing ever-increasingly until early adulthood. This developmental period is exploratory, motivating them to explore the world while at the same time presenting challenges to their well-being. For example, adolescents' risky choices, higher sensitivity to gains and losses, and perspective-taking are key decision-making components (Van Duijvenvoorde & Crone 2013). Thus, children's and adolescents' brains make predictions, too, and their brains become better at predicting as they age, but they will still make mistakes. As educators, we play a key role in helping students by understanding prediction's role in their behavior. Instead of considering what consequences or punishments a child needs, we should consider what experiences they need to shape and mature their brain.

STATE-DEPENDENT BRAIN FUNCTION

How is it that we are sometimes completely open to learning or processing new information, thinking, or reasoning, and at other times not? The functioning depends on the state of various parts of our brain; hence, another core concept of the Neurosequential Model is "state-dependent functioning" (see Figure 3.2). If the information entering the brainstem is registered as "safe," we will likely feel relaxed, safe, and calm—in other words, regulated. If our situation (classroom, staffroom, living room, playground) creates a sense of belonging and community, we feel connected with others. If these conditions are met, we have enough "bandwidth" available for higher-level thinking, planning, remembering, and reasoning—we are using our cortex.

"STATE"	CALM	ALERT	ALARM	FEAR	TERROR
DOMINANT BRAIN AREAS	CORTEX (DMN)	CORTEX (LIMBIC)	LIMBIC (DIENCEPHELON)	DIENCEPHELON (BRAINSTEM)	BRAINSTEM
Cognition	Abstract (creative)	Concrete (routine)	Emotional	Reactive	Reflexive
Functional IQ	120–100	110–90	100–80	90–70	80–60
Sense of time	Extended future	Days/Hours	Hours/Minutes	Minutes/Seconds	Loss of sense of time

Figure 3.2: State dependence: Sense of time, cognition, and functional IQ

There is much that can interfere with this pattern of brain function, especially when we are stressed (i.e., dysregulated). When we are dysregulated, remembering anything becomes harder, figuring out a clever response is more difficult, and paying attention to a classroom lesson or conversation can become impossible. Being oversensitized or overstimulated by a history of adverse childhood experiences or prolonged experiences such as being stuck in a refugee camp, the Covid-19 pandemic, or the chronic duress of a toxic workplace can profoundly impact our brain growth, development, and behavior.

When *calm*, we have access to our neocortex, the part of our brain that allows for abstract thinking and deeper reflection. We think and function with more access to the best parts of our executive functions. As our stress response increases to the *alert* state, our thinking becomes more concrete black-and-white. When the *alarm* state is activated (because of the stressors), the social-emotional limbic brain dominates, and rather than rational thought, our emotions drive our behaviors. When we enter into the *fear-terror* state, our fight-flight-freeze-faint-feign-flock responses are activated—we are controlled by these most primitive of responses. We cannot access our best selves, values, beliefs, or rational thinking in this state. Our focus shifts from being relational and reasoned to a complete focus on survival. The brainstem has become the brain's boss, protecting us from real or perceived danger.

When the brain is dysregulated, the lower parts of the brain are prioritized over the higher, more rational parts. In the second video in the series *Stress, Trauma, and the Brain: Insights for Educators*, Perry (2020) notes that if a person with an IQ of 130 is put under enough stress/duress, their IQ can decay temporarily by 10 to 20 points, and very quickly. This happens because the lower survival parts of our brain shut down the higher-thinking parts of our brain. This makes sense from an evolutionary perspective because "thinking" with your rational brain takes longer, and if the threat is immediate, it may end your life! People interviewed after a crisis often say, "I did not think; I acted!" We need our thinking brain to shut down in moments of threat so we do not get lost in thought. We get overtaken by action, which is what the threat calls us to do: to act!

Many of us are familiar with the experiences of panicking about something small and seeing how our behavior becomes almost silly. How many of us have spent ten minutes searching for our glasses in a panic only to find them on our heads? Many of us have also spent countless moments searching the house in a frenzy to find our cell phone, only to realize it is in our hands and we are currently using it. These experiences exemplify how stress impacts our functioning; hence the term state-dependent functioning.

APPLYING THIS KNOWLEDGE IN THE CLASSROOM

Imagine you are a ten-year-old child who did not sleep well last night while your parents were fighting. You wake up and help your younger sister prepare for school because your parents are passed out on the couch, and you are trying not to wake them. You finally make it to the bus, where other kids joke about how disheveled you look. You make it to school already exhausted, and your teacher expects you to take a math quiz. How well can you navigate all this, given your morning so far? You sit down for the quiz feeling antsy and have difficulty sitting still while you have been "shushed" for a zillionth time and threatened with punishment for not being quiet. You try to focus on the math, which is not making sense. It feels odd because you did fine with these same math problems yesterday; today, they look foreign to you. This is an example of state-dependent functioning in the classroom (see Figure 3.2).

While learning may be viewed as a simple exchange between a teacher's knowledge and a student's mind, the process is more complicated. The information (data) from the educator, like all other information coming into the brain, enters the student's brain via the brainstem. When considering the implications of state-dependent functioning in the classroom, it makes sense that students need to be regulated enough to learn—not only as individual learners but as a whole group. They need to feel connected relationally, and only then can they engage with what we are trying to teach.

This describes, very simply, Perry's regulate, relate, and then reason "rules" for the sequence of engagement and processing (see Figure 3.3). More importantly, *we* have to be regulated. Perry's three Rs rule (Regulate, Relate, and then Reason) is useful for remembering what to do and in what order.

When regulated, our bodies are balanced, and there is a sense of safety. In this state, we can be relational and seek to connect with other humans for a sense of belonging or connectedness. If we feel safe, with our basic needs addressed, and feel as if we belong, we can access our higher functions of reason and reflection.

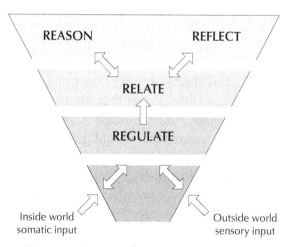

Figure 3.3: Sequence of engagement and processing

When we understand that the brain needs to be regulated and relational before we can be reasoned or reflective, we see that interventions we put into place must also follow this sequence. Our interventions need to start from the bottom up. When a child has issues with regulation of movement, that must be addressed before we address social and relational issues. If the child is struggling with social or relational issues, those need to be addressed before we deal with more cognitive issues.

ONCE IS NEVER ENOUGH: GETTING SMARTER WITH CONSEQUENCES

Suppose we want to be more mindful of effective ways to help children and young people change their behavior. In that case, we must understand that a single strategy designed to teach a new behavior or skill used once is unlikely to change the brain and behavior permanently. There is no such thing as a quick fix! Repetition is necessary. Focused, repetitive rehearsal and reinforcement (recognizing and acknowledging the growth) are needed. Indeed, Vince Lombardi (a famous American football coach) created this proverb: "Perfect practice makes perfect" (Lombardi, n.d.). While we doubt that Lombardi knew much about brain structure and function, he was referring to the ability of the brain to change—neuroplasticity at work!

It is not enough to tell students how to behave; we must get them to practice. Bruce Perry writes about *specificity*,[2] targeting that part of the brain involved in the skill we hope to develop. In simple terms, it means that to change a part of the brain or create a new pathway in the brain, we must target that specific part of the brain involved in the learning we want. One cannot learn to play the piano by watching someone play, as that would only involve the brain's visual centers and not the motor region involved in playing. To learn to play the piano, we need to involve and target those specific regions involved in playing: the motor regions, auditory senses, visual senses of seeing their hands on the keyboard, and the tactile sensations of having their fingers on the keys.

Daniel Reisel (2013, 2015), a neuroscientist who has studied the development of morality and empathy, writes that there are three

---

2   The neural network to be created or changed will need to be targeted with patterned, repetitive activation.

possible ways our brain might be re-wired, highlighting examples of neuroplasticity.

1. The first involves the concept of synaptic plasticity. You may have heard the phrase "cells that fire together, wire together." Repetition of behavior (or thought) enough times will create a more efficient transmission of neurotransmitters across the spaces that separate neurons in a particular pathway. Focused repetition over the same neural pathway also triggers the layering of myelin (a fatty sheath that surrounds a nerve cell), which scientists have found increases the speed and strength of electrical nerve impulses. We must be careful about our practices to avoid developing bad habits!

2. The second is neurogenesis, the birth of new brain cells as the brain renews itself. Reisel (p.59) states, "In some areas of the mammalian brain, more than 20 percent of cells are newly formed. Our brains are exquisitely sensitive to stress in our environment." The more stress, the less brain development, and the less the brain can adapt, which causes more stress.

3. The third is epigenetics. Epigenetics refers to how DNA is read and expressed in our bodies and what genes are active or not at a given moment. For example, internalized stress is thought to cause epigenetic changes that may play a role in the development of such conditions as attention deficit hyperactivity disorder (ADHD) or depression. This is vital to understand if we are to make sense of the behavior of children and young people in our classrooms who have been exposed to chronic neglect and abuse and the associated flood of stress hormones such as glucocorticoids and adrenaline. Over time, this can alter the expression of our genes and result, for example, in low impulse control.

USE IT OR LOSE IT

By now, it would be no surprise to learn that brain growth is use-dependent. If a part of the brain is repeatedly used, it grows by creating new connections and laying down new neural pathways through synaptic plasticity and neurogenesis. Think London cab drivers. To get a license to drive the famous cabs, the applicant must have memorized the streets of inner London without reference to GPS. A cabbie's hippocampus is larger than average because of the work required to memorize the maps. If a part of the brain is not utilized, it will not grow; thus, "use it or lose it."

At the risk of repeating ourselves, this is why "perfect practice makes perfect." With each focused, patterned repetition, the axons of the neurons involved in this new pathway develop thicker myelin, increasing the speed and efficiency of the electrical impulse. Remember Dan Reisel's "cells that fire together, wire together," the common term to describe the improved efficiency of neurotransmitters. Think of a truck driven over a paddock with shoulder-high grass just once. The grass will return to upright as the truck moves on. If this same track is used repeatedly, the track will eventually grow no grass. If the track is unused for months or years, it will regrow the vegetation as it was—use it or lose it in action! This is another argument for moving away from behavioristic approaches using punishment and rewards and expecting these strategies to create new behavior habits. Punishment and rewards are not empowered to do this work in our brains.

REALISTIC EXPECTATIONS OF CHANGE

This is a great place to talk about realistic behavior change in children. Adults tend to have unrealistic expectations of behavior change in that we expect behavior change at 100 percent overnight or with just one punitive sanction. One suspension or reward is not likely enough to change behavior from 0 to 100 percent. When our attempts fail, we do not acknowledge the failure of our unrealistic intervention; we blame the child for not trying hard enough.

In the United States and other Western countries, a multi-million-dollar self-help industry tries to help adults struggling to lose weight, balance their checkbooks, or change unwanted habits. Books like *Atomic Habits*, *Change Anything*, and *The Power of Habit* try to give people the skills and understanding to make better choices, yet many programs are still insufficient to get folks to quit smoking or lose weight. Despite adults' best efforts, they often find it hard to make changes. We tend to overestimate "willpower," which is not that powerful! Adults who expect change to happen immediately in children might examine their own behavior change challenges.

Oddly, those same adults expect children to change overnight or with a simple "talking to." More realistic would be helping them take baby steps. Maybe we do not get Billy to attend class on time every day. Maybe we get him to be late three out of five days instead of five out of five. Maybe Deshawn does not always turn in his work, yet he went from no work to two assignments completed this week. Small incremental changes are still changes, and maybe this is what this child can do right now with the stress they are facing. Do not lower your expectations; keep them realistic. When we remember that all learning is the creation of new neural connections, we see why change is hard. It takes repetition! It takes work to make new habits. It takes time to learn new things, including behavior.

CENTRAL IDEAS

★ The brain is undeveloped at birth. Children gain more executive functions as the brain develops, allowing them to regulate their body, mind, and behavior. Our brains are constantly adapting and changing in response to our environment.

★ The brain processes all information from the bottom up. Lower parts of the brain focusing on survival will always dominate over higher, more reasoned parts when humans are under threat or stress.

★ Our brains work on predictions made from sensory information mixed with past experiences. These predictions can be in error when humans have more negative experiences than positive ones.

★ Functions of the brain are dependent on our nervous system state. When one loses access to the higher functions, stress or threat increases. The more regulated and safer we feel, the more access we have to higher functions.

★ Behavior change is brain change. Making changes takes time and repetition, and they rarely happen overnight.

REFLECTION QUESTIONS

✓ Think of the last time you knew something you couldn't bring to mind. What was the state of your nervous system at that time?

✓ When do you get your best ideas? What are you doing when those ideas come to you? What is the state of your nervous system when those ideas come to you?

✓ Typically, we have seen children's behavior as a matter of choices or boundary testing. The level of "thinking" required for those choices and reasoning is mostly unavailable to children with an undeveloped cortex. What changes for you when you learn that behavior is more about nervous system states?

✓ Name a habit or behavior you have been trying to change. What struggles have you had with changing your behavior as an adult? What would support your efforts to change your behavior? How does knowing that change your approach to helping children change their behavior?

✓ When you think of changing a child's behavior, can you identify your goals of intervention? What experiences does this child require to develop the executive functions they will need? How can you provide those experiences in positive, moderate, and controllable ways the brain is open to learning from?

✓ When looking at Figure 3.2 on state dependence, what do you notice about your ability to function under stress? What could schools do to support educators in having more access to the higher regions of their brain?

Our next chapter will dive deeper into dysregulation, self-regulation, and co-regulation. These are the important tools that allow us to support children, starting with our ability as adults to be aware of the contagious nature of the state of our nervous system.

CHAPTER 4

Regulation and Co-Regulation

In this chapter, we dive into the concept of regulation. It cannot be stated enough how important this core concept is to a trauma-informed educator. It starts with us because children learn to regulate their systems in no other way except through co-regulation. As adults, we do this instinctively for infants and small children. We hear and learn what each small cry means from an infant and tend to those needs. We feed them, change their diapers, or rock and bounce them to soothe their cries. Sadly, we often fail to realize that when they continue to ask for our help, we see it as misbehavior rather than communication. We hope this chapter, if not this whole book, will change that lens.

WHAT IS REGULATION?

When we are "regulated," it simply means that our body, including our nervous system, is balanced. We've had enough sleep, enough to nourish us, and our bodies have had the proper amount of movement required to keep us balanced. Dr. Bruce Perry writes:

> Regulation is also about being in balance. We have many different systems that are continuously monitoring our body and the outside world to make sure we're safe and in balance—that we have enough food, water, oxygen. When we're regulated, these systems have what they need. (Perry & Winfrey 2021, p.48)

Regulation is not like having an on or off light switch; it is more of a continuum. We move from various states of regulation to dysregulation, depending on how out of balance we have become (see "State-dependent brain function" in Chapter 3). Dysregulation can arise in response to various circumstances from the inside world (i.e., interoception), like being hungry, tired, or thirsty, and the outside world (i.e., the five senses), like threats, toxic stress, environmental stress, and bad news.

FIVE DOMAINS OF REGULATION

According to Shanker and Barker (2017) in their book *Self-Reg: How to Help Your Child (and You) Break the Stress Cycle and Successfully Engage with Life*, there are five domains of regulation. The first is *biological* regulation. This is a child's ability to control and regulate their physical self. This is about a child learning to understand the sensory world in and around them and respond appropriately (knowing when it's time to go to the bathroom or get a drink). Next is *emotional* regulation. This type of regulation allows children to experience positive emotions enjoyably. It is also the capacity to manage intense or overwhelming positive or negative emotions. Then, we have *cognitive* regulation. Dr. Bruce Perry often calls this top-down regulation. This is a child's ability to focus their attention and block out distractions. Another is *social* regulation. This is a child's ability to read and manage social cues. These abilities allow children to make and maintain friendships. The last domain is *prosocial* regulation, a child's ability to empathize emotionally and cognitively with others. This ability allows them to take an interest in others' emotions, show care when others are not at their best, and share in others' joy.

As stated earlier, our functioning and ability to self-regulate depend on our arousal state, ranging from calm, alert, and alarm to fear and terror. We lose our higher thinking and reasoning in response to dysregulation as the focus of the brain's energy moves to survival. Dr. Lori Desautels (2023) explains it this way:

> A regulated nervous system is prepared for cognitive and mental tasks. A regulated nervous system is ready to parent with all the challenges we encounter. A regulated nervous system is ready to lead. But we cannot always find calm regulation; acknowledging when we are dysregulated is critical in our journey toward well-being. (p.86)

Our first experiences of being fully regulated happen intrauterine. The umbilical cord supplies nutrients, oxygen, and a stable supply of hormones, keeping us cozy, safe, and warm. We hear and feel the rhythm of our mother's heart beating at about 60–80 beats per minute, while simultaneously hearing the diaphragm tapping as the mother breathes. On top of that symphony, we also hear the swooshing of blood moving through the body. These rhythmic, patterned, and repetitive sounds lay the groundwork for music. This also lays the groundwork for why those three qualities in the environment can regulate the lower parts of our brains. We associate patterned, rhythmic, and repetitive sounds with having our basic needs met. Because the associations of rhythm, repetition, and patterns are deep in our memories, these can help regulate our nervous systems.

TYPES OF REGULATION
Self-regulation

- *Bottom-up regulation (somatosensory/self-soothing):* This is our primary type of regulation as it mimics our intrauterine (prenatal) experiences. It involves patterned, rhythmic, and repetitive activities, such as walking, biking, drawing, coloring, dancing, or running. It can be seen in some younger children who rock themselves, or babies and the very young who suck their thumbs. We see it when we notice foot shaking, knee bouncing, or even chewing gum. For some students, it may also involve picking at their skin, clothes, or bedsheets while they sleep. Other examples include spinning in a chair, tapping a pen or pencil on the desk, drumming on the desk, kicking the seat in front, and so on. Many bottom-up regulation tactics in children, such as stimming, are for sensory input by the brainstem or the motor brain to satisfy the need for movement. Bottom-up regulation can also look like a fidgety child. For other children, it may be about limiting or controlling sensory input they find overwhelming.

- *Top-down regulation (cortical modulation):* This is our secondary type of regulation. This is when the cortex, our higher-thinking region, calms the brain's lower regions. This is a slower process as the information has to travel through the layers of the brain up to the top and then down again. A classic example of top-down regulation is potty training or using the restroom—we know this comes with practice over time. There is a catch with top-down regulation, and that is that it is state-dependent. We can only utilize this option when we are calm enough to access it. The deeper into the continuum of dysregulation, the less likely top-down modulation is available to us.

Because children lack a fully developed cortex, their top-down regulation will be difficult, especially under stress. Regulated children behave better because they can access higher thinking; therefore, top-down regulation is possible. Improving student behavior involves creating environments that promote safety and relationships to help regulate students, giving them access to top-down regulation.

- *Dissociation (immobilization):* This is a universal type of regulation and one of the oldest responses to threats or stress in human evolution. Unlike our "fight or flight" responses to threat, stress, or adversity, our parasympathetic nervous system shuts us down via a particular nerve called the dorsal vagus branch of the vagal nerve (Dana 2020; Porges 2017). Our bodies do this when the threat is overwhelming, and we cannot outrun or fight it. Instead, our system prepares for the pain. Our blood pressure and heart rate may drop, and our bodies may be flooded with painkillers (i.e., endorphins and natural opioids). Dr. Bruce Perry explains:

    For babies and very young children, dissociation is a very common adaptive strategy; fighting or fleeing won't protect you, but "disappearing" might. You learn to escape into your inner world. You dissociate. And over time, your capacity to retreat to that inner world—safe, free, in-control—increases. (Perry & Winfrey 2021, p.59)

- *External regulation:* Another way humans regulate their nervous systems is through external sources such as drugs, alcohol, food, sex, and the distractions of mindless cell phone use. Many of these activities and substances positively activate our internal reward systems, helping regulate (soothe) the body. These activities allow the brain to release some feel-good chemicals like dopamine and serotonin. These chemicals are part of the core regulatory networks in our brains. Many individuals who have experienced trauma, including chaotic, unpredictable environments, may find that these substances and activities quiet their systems and allow them some temporary relief from distress.

This brings us back to the conversation about our personal journey to becoming a trauma-informed restorative educator. It is hoped that it is obvious that meeting our basic needs and wellness is key to keeping us, as the "adults in the room," in a regulated state where we can support students. We are of little use to a dysregulated child if we, too, are dysregulated. You cannot share a "calm" that you do not have. To go further, you will share that state when you are dysregulated or even escalated, too! "Our emotions are contagious" (Brummer & Thorsborne 2020, p.56).

Co-regulation

As already flagged, regulation is really about the state of our nervous system. If regulated, our needs are met, and we can access the higher systems in our brains. We reach these states through bottom-up approaches, top-down approaches, dissociative states, or outside sources like food, sex, drugs, or even shopping. Children do not develop the skills needed to regulate their nervous systems independently; they learn regulation through the repeated experiences of being co-regulated by an attuned and grounded adult.

As Ginger Healy (2023) writes in her book *Regulation and Co-regulation: Accessible Neuroscience and Connection Strategies that Bring Calm into the Classroom*:

Co-regulation is when a child and a nurturing, reliable caregiver share a sense of safety and engage in warm and responsive interactions to learn how to soothe and manage distressing emotions. The adult provides intentional modeling of the regulated state, and the child learns self-regulation. It helps the child understand their feelings, thoughts, and subsequent behavior. (p.41)

Lori Desautels (2023) defines co-regulation this way: "This process is our biological priority, as human beings are social creatures who need one another to find feelings of safety and connection" (p.286). We should not wait for a child to become dysregulated to focus on their regulation. When we see regulation as something we can teach them to maintain, we will have fewer fires to put out because we didn't allow the fire to start in the first place.

Located in the Appendices, there are some examples of regulation and co-regulation that echo this advice—moving whole classes, small groups, or individuals through patterned, rhythmic, and repetitive exercises before the lessons start to help them become and stay calm so that they can access the higher centers of their brain for learning or problem-solving.

As we are social animals, the human nervous system states are contagious (Brummer & Thorsborne 2020). This can be both a curse and a blessing. On the positive side, it allows us to share a sense of grounded calm that others may perceive in us as cues of safety. On the negative, when we are dysregulated, we share that sense of alarm or threat system activation with others. Our students who have experienced sensitization of their nervous systems through trauma, toxic stress, or adversity may be more attuned and alert to the cues of unsafety in others. This means adults with dysregulated nervous systems cannot regulate students needing safety; they can only give what they have.

This fact requires some honesty on the part of adults in educational settings. We cannot always be a superhuman hero/heroine swooping in to save our students. We must be honest with ourselves when we cannot regulate a struggling student because our nervous system is too out of balance. To cope with highly stressful situations—and let's face it, working with children and young people is sometimes like this—we must look after ourselves. We cannot do this work if we are running on empty. Read Chapter 5 on wellness and regulation for more about this.

Debra Wilson (2023), in her book *Polyvagal Path to Joyful Learning: Transforming Classrooms One Nervous System at a Time*, detailing the use of polyvagal theory[1] in classrooms, lists seven principles and habits for becoming more successful at regulating our brains. Her advice (with a little addition from us here and there) includes the need to:

- befriend our nervous system so that we know what's happening when we move in and out of a regulated state

- notice situations when we feel safe or unsafe

- understand that our regulation comes first and how to tap into internal or external resources to achieve that

- notice that when discord occurs in our relationships with others, we have to tap into our "calm" and move into the repair space

- view conflict as an opportunity

- use our restorative skills and stay curious, not furious

- be adaptable in calming ourselves, given the context and situation

- stay organized using lists, post-it notes, and other reminders to reduce our cognitive load—this will also lower our stress levels

- stay curious about what's happening to our brain state and do this for others

- take a break and do something joyful.

It will be even more important for us not only to use strategies that regulate, relate, and allow for reason with students but also to stay in touch with the *why* of regulation. We want to allow a child access to the best parts of their brain if we expect them to learn or behave at their best. The why is just as important as the how, and needs to inform the *how* of helping a student regulate. Table 4.1 summarizes what co-regulation is and is not.

---

1 Polyvagal theory offers precise science to understand how the vagus nerve, one part of the autonomic system, connects the brain to the heart and the organs of the belly. It has two main branches—the dorsal vagus and the ventral vagus—both involved in our capacity to respond to safety or danger (www.windhorseimh.org/being-polyvagal-the-polyvagal-theory-explained).

Table 4.1: Co-regulation

What it is not	What it is
Rewarding bad behavior	Soothing nervous system dysregulation
Demand for compliance/obedience	Relational regulation
Showing off our power/authority	Sharing our sense of safety
Permissive/free-range children and youths	Putting boundaries/structure in place
Manipulation	Helping students connect to calm
Aggressive control	Assertive compassion
Focused on changing behaviour	Focused on changing nervous system state
Sending the child away	Holding presence and space for the child
Assumption of choice in behavior	Assumption of struggle with emotions
Controlling bad behaviors through threats or incentives (*other-directed motivation*)	Influencing future choices through cues of safety (*self-directed motivation*)
Focused on adult expectations	Focused on the current needs of the child
Escalation based on the child's hostility	Absorbing the child's hostility and sharing calm

Adapted from Healy (2023, p.42).

Using Dr. Bruce Perry's regulate, relate, and reason mantra (Chapter 3), it is clear that any approach to problem-solving must first create a space for becoming calm, then use the *connect before correct* approach to ease into the dialogue about what has gone wrong. Only then can we begin any reasoning—the restorative conversation.

CENTRAL IDEAS

★ Regulation is a state of our bodies being in balance. It means that our basic needs are met, and we feel a sense of safety and belonging.

★ There are five domains of regulation: biological (body), cognitive (mind), emotional (heart), social, and prosocial.

★ Humans can regulate four main ways: bottom-up, top-down, dissociation, or outside sources.

★ We are social herd-like creatures whose nervous system states are contagious.

★ Co-regulation occurs when a regulated human shares their sense of felt safety with another human.

★ Keeping our students regulated in the classroom improves behavior.

REFLECTION QUESTIONS

✓ When do you feel the most regulated in your day? When do you feel the least regulated?

✓ What is your go-to for bottom-up regulation? Foot shaking? Gum chewing? Pencil tapping?

✓ What bottom-up regulation strategies do you notice in your students? Is it different at different times of the school day? Are some students more regulated than others?

✓ When you think about your typical behavior interventions, do you regulate or dysregulate your students? Do your interventions follow the sequence of engagement—regulate, relate, and reason?

✓ When you reflect on the last time you were frustrated or angry, what was the state of your nervous system? How well did you do at coming up with solutions?

✓ Have you noticed some children in your classroom with glassy eyes, spaced out, or seeming to not be "here" in the moment? What is your strategy to check in or help regulate their systems?

✓ When reflecting on Table 4.1: Co-Regulation, which side of the table feels most "normal" for you as an educator? Parent? Leader?

Chapter 5 discusses ways to think about wellness and its links to our capacity to regulate that around several interrelated concepts. We cannot do this work with regulation, self-regulation, and co-regulation unless we have the right equipment—our health and well-being and healthy connections with others. Later, in Chapter 6, we expand our thinking about how we might work with our students and classes to address the need for large group regulation so that a room full of students can be engaged in learning.

CHAPTER 5

Wellness: Improving Our Capacity for Regulation

Over the last several years, and certainly through the Covid-19 lock-downs, some people have weaponized "self-care" as code for "learn how to take care of *yourself.*"

While school administration may intend to help with the stress by offering workshops on mindfulness or suggesting other activities about how to take care of yourself, they often have little capacity to lessen the stressors (the events that cause us to experience stress), so their response is typical: "Here is how to take care of the stress." Sadly, no amount of yoga, meditation, or daily tips for better "self-care," such as soaking in a hot bath or writing in a gratitude journal, is comprehensive enough to regulate the nervous systems of educators trapped in environments that pile on stressors.

This chapter will examine sleep, nutrition, and exercise/move-ment—three pillars of wellness that can aid our ability to regulate our nervous system. We explore the significance of relational health and mindfulness and their contribution to wellness. If we are unwell, our ability to stay regulated will be reduced. When we enter our classrooms in a dysregulated state, there is no way we can effectively manage dysregulated students. Engaging proactively in wellness practices that support better nervous system functioning is essential to enhancing our health and productivity.

WELL-BEING AND WELLNESS

Our well-being can be described as a positive orientation about life going well, feeling good, and functioning effectively. It does not mean feeling good all the time, never functioning less than optimally at times, or the absence of painful emotions such as disappointment, failure, and grief, which are normal parts of life that we must learn to manage effectively to promote long-term well-being (Huppert 2009). We can gauge our well-being by having a sense of purpose and realizing how much control we have over our lives and our emotions, confidence, and engagement with interests, affection, and positive relationships (Ruggeri *et al.* 2020; Ryan & Deci 2020). Our well-being can be compromised when there are factors that are extreme or long-lasting and interfere with our ability to function effectively in our daily lives.

Wellness is an important construct influenced by multiple dimensions that support our overall well-being. Specifically, whole-person (i.e., holistic) wellness emphasizes addressing the various dimensions of our being, including physical, mental, emotional, relational, intellectual, spiritual, and vocational (Stoner & Stoner 2020). These dimensions each link to the other, and each dimension of wellness is linked to key areas of well-being, such as our autonomy and interests, affection, positive relationships, and a sense of purpose. Keeping our wellness dimensions balanced is always important, but it is essential when we face stressful times.

Both wellness and well-being operate on a continuum, with illness or dismay on one end and wellness and optimal well-being on the other. We all operate somewhere along this continuum at all points of our lives. The signs and symptoms we experience as part of an illness, disease, or dismay are the *mind and body's attempts to solve a problem*. For example, considering our emotional and mental well-being, people often lack signs and symptoms of a physical illness, yet psychologically, they are bored, depressed, anxious, and generally unhappy. The mind and body do much of their work below our level of consciousness; signs and symptoms of a disease are messages from our subconscious to our conscious that our mind and body are not working as they should and that something needs to be done. Our brain and the rest of our nervous system are trying to balance themselves and the rest of the body.

We want to develop mindful awareness of what it "feels like" when we are well and when we are not. As a constantly evolving construct, wellness does not exist in a vacuum, nor is it a static state of our well-being; we do not get and stay well. High-level wellness consists of a belief system and values that guide us toward our best well-being. It means something different at every stage of life, and just like well-being, it is individually defined. Living our lives with curiosity and mindful awareness is the cornerstone of high-level wellness and well-being.

TAKING CARE OF OUR OWN WELLNESS

A self-care approach to wellness is creating action (Nagoski & Nagoski 2020). It is a conscious, self-directed, and evolving process (National Wellness Institute 2023). It includes developing a transformational mindset, learning to set realistic and achievable wellness goals, developing personalized action plans and strategies to overcome barriers, and breaking down goals into smaller manageable steps that promote success. These approaches suggest that self-care practices are not a one-time approach to wellness. They are ongoing practices embedded in the various wellness dimensions that meet our physical, mental, and emotional needs, help to reduce our vulnerability to unpleasant emotions, and may improve our overall well-being. In other words, self-care consists of the specific choices and behaviors that, over time, lead to improved wellness. No matter where we are in life, we are constantly changing and can allow ourselves to move toward a positive state of well-being (Travis & Ryan 2004). A self-care approach to wellness is about having the self-knowledge and mental and emotional flexibility to make the best choices for our health and well-being, which may differ throughout our lives. Ideal well-being is a journey, not a destination, that requires frequent reassessing and rebalancing as we consider what forms of self-care are best for us.

THE BODY BUDGET

The body is a collection of systems that work together to serve a common purpose—the prime operative being survival, reproduction, and growth. Imagine these body systems working together like a financial budget, always trying to stay balanced without surpluses or deficits; our nervous system keeps track of this delicate balancing act, calculating everything our bodies need to stay balanced. Barrett

(2017) refers to this as our body's budget, and one of our brain's most important functions is to reach and maintain homeostasis. Homeostasis is our body's natural ability to regulate various physiological processes to keep its internal states steady and balanced. Considering the body budget is a useful way of balancing the issues affecting our well-being. It helps us to better appreciate the two-way link between our mind and body so we can take a holistic approach to understanding and improving our physical and mental well-being.

Balancing the body's budget is done through our brain's ability to use prediction to navigate the world. Barrett (2017), in her groundbreaking book *How Emotions are Made: The Secret Life of the Brain*, explains predictions this way:

> ...trapped within the skull, with only past experiences as a guide, your brain makes *predictions*. We usually think of predictions as statements about the future, like "It's going to rain tomorrow" or "The Red Sox will win the World Series" or "You will meet a tall, dark stranger." But here, I'm focusing on predictions on a microscopic scale as millions of neurons talk to one another. These neural conversations try to anticipate every fragment of sight, sound, smell, taste, and touch that you will experience, and every action you will take. These predictions are your brain's best guesses of what's going on in the world around you, and how to deal with it to keep you alive and well. (p.59)

In managing the body budget, our brain uses our current affect and interoception mixed with sensory data from the outside world (i.e., anything we see, hear, smell, taste, and touch) and what our mind imagines could do us harm. This helps us make meaning of and predict what resources our body has and needs to stay balanced in our moment-to-moment existence. For example, everything from the amount of oxygen we might need to perform a task, to how much glucose our body will need to go dancing, to how fast our heart should beat to get oxygen-carrying blood flowing to the right places it predicted it would need. Your body budget works as you sit or stand while reading this book. Your brain is predicting how much salt, glucose, and water are necessary for your physical energy needs, such as body position, and for your brain to interpret the light waves entering through your eyes, so these words become a visual representation you can understand and use to your benefit. The efficiency of this prediction system depends on how well the body is managed and maintained. Though below our level of consciousness, this is part of wellness.

Human beings are holistic (Boyes-Watson & Pranis 2015); we can only be understood as the sum of our parts. Yet often, mostly due to culture, we divide and separate these parts of ourselves. We often see our mental health as separate from our physical health. We see our professional selves as separate from our personal selves. Sadly, many of us fail to make the connections between our various dimensions of wellness, such as physical well-being, and spiritual, emotional, or inner well-being. We sometimes fail to see ourselves holistically, so we don't see the impact on our emotional wellness from the food we eat, how we move our bodies, and how much rest we allow ourselves. Each of these impacts our ability to balance the body budget, sometimes profoundly. When the budget is in balance, we are regulated. When regulated, we can offer that sense of grounding to students and colleagues. Dr. Bruce Perry backs this up when he writes, "Balance is the core of health. We feel and function best when our body's systems are in balance, and when we're in balance with friends, family, and community, and nature" (Perry & Winfrey 2021, p.48).

NERVOUS SYSTEM WELLNESS

To understand how the systems that affect wellness are interconnected, we need to start by examining our nervous system. The brain, together with the rest of our nervous system, is considered the master control system of the entire body. Although our brain supports its homeostasis and controls our psychological processes, the nervous system is a physical structure throughout the body (via nerves) that orchestrates and regulates other body systems. Our mind and body function more efficiently when our brain and nervous system are healthier. While stress is an everyday experience, and there is no way of escaping it, an overloaded, ill-functioning brain and nervous system cannot handle sustained physical or emotional stress. When laden with physical symptoms like pain, our minds and bodies become fraught with feelings of overwhelm and other psychological distress. Eventually, this distress will lead to other physical symptoms like headaches. Chronic stress can affect every tissue and organ in the body, leading to many physical and mental illnesses.

With a direct connection between a healthy brain and nervous system and our ability to think creatively and feel clearly, there is no question that being our healthiest depends on the best nervous system performance. An overloaded nervous system creates malfunction in our minds and bodies. If we are not "well," we cannot improve how our body responds to stress. Recall from Chapter 4, in our discussion about dysregulation, when our nervous system is regulated, we can access our thinking mind and are ready to take on our daily tasks and prepare for tomorrow. We acknowledge when we are dysregulated because it is critical in our journey toward well-being (Desautels 2023).

Stressors and the stress response

The American Psychological Association (2023a) defines a *stressor* as any internal or external event, force, or condition resulting in a physical or emotional *stress response* that requires the affected individual's adjustment or strategies for coping. Thus, *stress* is the *response* our mind and body experience as the result of a stressor and is "a normal reaction to everyday pressures but can become unhealthy when it upsets [our] day-to-day functioning" (American Psychological Association 2023b) and includes physical, mood, behavioral, and cognitive responses to our perception of various situations (i.e., real or perceived), with examples of these reactions shown in Table 5.1.

Table 5.1: How stress manifests itself

Physical effects	Sweaty palms
	Tension in shoulders
	Dry mouth
	Increased heart and respiratory rates
	Skin rashes
Mood effects	What typically interests you no longer does
Behavioral effects	Engaging in excess activity or not doing anything
	Body-focused repetitive regulating behaviors (e.g., nail biting, fidgeting)

Cognitive effects	Difficulty in making decisions, large or small
	Unable to concentrate (see "State-dependent brain functioning" in Chapter 3)

Stressors can be anything we see, hear, smell, touch, taste, or imagine that disrupts the body's homeostasis and generally fall into two broad categories: physiological (e.g., hunger, chronic illness, injury, pain) and psychological, including events, situations, and individuals that make us feel stressed and uneasy (e.g., difficulties at home, financial worry, concerns about physical safety, self-criticism, and, as we mentioned earlier, the Covid-19 pandemic). As educators, work-related stressors include concerns about school organization, job demands, work resources, and social-emotional factors that allow one to feel competent (or not) in their profession (Greenberg, Brown, & Abenavoli 2016; Karbowski 2022). We would add that constant and prolonged worry about managing the struggles students face and the symptoms that show up in their behavior—that we are expected to be able to manage—also amounts to a stressor. Think about those students who come to school hungry or have sensory issues (e.g., noise, lighting, dirt) and how difficult it must be for them.

When we encounter a stressor, the limbic system in our brain acts like a command center and must perceive it as one and assign a salience level; that is, whether to pay it any attention (see Chapters 3 and 8). This is a very quick process. If the stressor is recognized as distressing, the brain elicits a corresponding stress response—what we know as fight, flight, or freeze—regardless of whether the stressor is a real or perceived threat. The result is a cascade of stress hormones released throughout the body, like cortisol and adrenaline/epinephrine, which produce physiological changes that raise our heart rate, constrict our blood vessels, and raise our blood sugar to give us the energy to respond to a situation.

The stress response is adaptive for most stressors as it prepares the body to manage a stressor's challenges. Some stressors are *acute* or brief events such as a heated argument, getting stuck in a traffic jam, or having an ill child. Our stress response may include sweaty palms, increased heart rate, and a short-lived psychological response, such as concern. However, our mind and body return to homeostasis quickly once the stressor is removed. *Acute episodic stress* is acute stress with some regularity, like a looming work deadline or occasionally taking on too much responsibility. If we feel rushed, always late, constantly worrying, we may experience acute episodic stress. An acute episodic stress response is like acute stress, in addition to being physically and mentally exhausting. We may feel under pressure or that things are always going wrong. We may experience trouble communicating thoughts and feelings. Again, once the stressor is removed, we typically regain homeostasis. Refer to Table 5.1 to see how stress manifests in our mind and body.

With acute or acute episodic stress, while we may not be able to control the things that cause us stress, we can develop better skills to deal with stress by accessing the cortex (i.e., top-down regulation) to manage our response better, leading to better health and productivity. With most acute and acute episodic stressors, we can either respond to a stressor negatively (i.e., distress) or positively (i.e., eustress), meaning we can view it as a negative challenge that can become paralyzing, leaving us feeling helpless and overwhelmed, or we can create a mental shift and view it with curiosity as a challenge for opportunity and growth. With this being said, accessing the cortex to manage your response is a form of top-down regulation (see Chapters 3 and 4), which can be a struggle for anyone experiencing chronic stress or a history of life events resulting in trauma. Stressors will be filtered through every experience one has ever had—traumatic or not—and accessing the cortex is necessary for top-down regulation to adapt to stressors effectively.

The stressor's timing and intensity also matter, as does its predictability. Perry and Szalavitz (2006) write that "resilience or vulnerability to stress depend upon a person's neural system's tolerance following earlier experience" (p.40) and the key to a "resilient, flexible, stress response" that can make us "stronger and more functionally capable" is "through moderate, predictable challenges" so that our "stress response systems are activated moderately" (p.41). When the stress we experience is felt or perceived as intense, such as prolonged chronic stress (e.g., high-pressure job, financial difficulties, a challenging relationship, toxic workplace stress) or trauma, the response is maladaptive and detrimental to our mental and physical health. As Perry and Szalavitz (2006, p.41) state, "the pattern and intensity of experience matter. If a system is overloaded—worked beyond capacity—the result can be profound deterioration, disorganization and dysfunction" to our "brain's stress networks when confronted with traumatic stress."

Concerning the dimensions of wellness mentioned earlier, stress affects every dimension of our wellness and well-being, as it affects every tissue and organ in our bodies. Our brain and the rest of our nervous system work to keep themselves and all of our body systems in homeostasis to survive and function optimally (American Psychological Association 2023b). Thus, our nervous system can become overloaded as we struggle with unhealthy stress—for some, this happens nearly daily. The key to managing stress is to be mindful of how we feel in the present moment of a stress response; when we describe our stress, we become aware of this in our body's physiology and our brains and minds (psychology).

Stressors are relative to us at an individual level; no two people will experience the same stressor in the same way. While a stressor can be anything we interpret as negative or threatening, some people experience it as stressful and traumatic. For others, it may be deeply stressful but not traumatic. In others, it has no effect. This may be due to genetics and life experiences (Siegel 2020, pp.49–53). We may inherit the effects of trauma from previous generations (i.e., epigenetics), and early life adversity, stress, and childhood trauma can affect our lifelong mental and physical health. While there are common elements to events and situations that create stress for everyone, as we previously discussed, any individual's stress reactions are filtered through their previous life experiences. For example, an individual reaction to a stressor (a car backfiring) can sometimes be traced back to traumatic events (gun fire in war). People who were neglected or abused as children tend to be particularly vulnerable to stress. Our maladaptive stress response builds over time. The key to preventing maladaptive stress responses is identifying and addressing signs of stress early on and continuously (refer to Table 5.1 to review the various ways stress affects the mind and body). When we do not deal with the stress productively, we are more likely to experience maladaptation with a prolonged, chronically dysregulated nervous system. Some examples of the maladaptive responses we may have to prolonged, chronic stress include:

- fatigue and sleep issues
- repeated periods of forgetfulness or trouble concentrating
- loss of interest in hobbies and activities like exercise
- appetite and weight issues
- emotional responses
- depression and anxiety
- intimacy concerns/decreased libido.

Understanding the stress cycle

We live in a world of stressors and stress; they are woven into our everyday experiences. We cannot escape either. One acute incident can stimulate our nervous system into flight or fight mode; however, as discussed earlier, our bodies typically return to homeostasis once the stressor is gone. Acute episodic, prolonged chronic, and traumatic events build stress over time. If we do not find a way to relieve the pent-up stress in our bodies, we stay stressed, and our lives are not built to live this way. When we don't effectively manage any stress, especially prolonged stress, we do a disservice to our mental and physical health (refer to the list above). But there are two things that we can do to mitigate the events in our lives that cause stress and our body's physiological experience of the stress. First, we can acknowledge that many stressors are unavoidable and uncontrollable—meaning, we recognize the stressor for what it is and determine what we can reasonably do about it that is within our control. Second, we can realize that what is in our control is the ability to expel the charged energy that builds throughout the day so that our minds and bodies can return to homeostasis—or what Emily and Amelia Nagoski (2020) call *completing the stress cycle*. In their book *Burnout: The Secret to Unlocking the Stress Cycle*, Emily and Amelia Nagoski discuss what causes burnout, what it does to our bodies, and how we can move through the emotional exhaustion accompanying prolonged chronic stress.

Stress has a cycle; it has a beginning, middle, and end, and the problem most of us have is when we get stuck in the middle.

Completing the stress cycle is how we can deal with the stress we experience from day-to-day stressful events to keep it from building up. Even after we've left our jobs for the day or walked away from a heated argument, it is still possible that our minds and bodies are stuck in the middle stage of the stress cycle. Even though the stressor may be gone, we may not have dealt with the adrenaline and cortisol built up in our body from that single event or the events throughout the day, weeks, or months. After a heated argument is over or we quit that toxic job, our mind may still be ruminating, and our body's physical reactions are present days, weeks, months, or years after the event. Emily and Amelia Nagoski write that because we tend to "deny, ignore, or suppress [our] stress response...most of us are walking around with decades of incomplete stress response cycles simmering away in our chemistry, just waiting for a chance to complete" (2020, p.11). So, while the stressor may have been left behind, the stress is not.

The stress that builds up in our bodies may be prevented—or at least managed—by changing our diet and nutrition, exercising, and getting enough sleep (more on this later). We can complete the stress cycle with proven methods to reduce or eliminate the daily build-up of stress hormones and allow our mind and body to be more at ease. Emily and Amelia Nagoski write that our body cannot tell the difference between the stressors we experience; it only knows, based on a degree of assigned valence, that we are experiencing a stressful event, so norepinephrine, epinephrine and cortisol, and other stress hormones are released into the blood in response to physical or emotional stress. They suggest speaking your body's language— using breathing and exercise to calm your nervous system (Nagoski & Nagoski 2020, p.15). While they offer many suggestions for completing the stress cycle, including positive social interaction, a good deep belly laugh, offering and receiving affection, crying, and being creative, there are two nervous system regulatory approaches that are most effective. These are daily exercise lasting from 20 to 60 minutes (more on this later) and breathing techniques where we slowly inhale for a count of five, hold our breath for a count of five, and then exhale for a count of ten, and repeat five times. During the slow exhale, we often feel the stress leaving our bodies (Nagoski & Nagoski 2020). Both exercise and breathing are bottom-up approaches to relieving stress. Emily and Amelia Nagoski say that you will know (and no doubt you already have experienced this) when you experience a "shift in mood or mental state or physical tension, as you breathe more deeply and your thoughts relax" (2020, p.21).

THREE PILLARS OF WELLNESS

So, two questions arise: "What do we need to do to keep our nervous system healthy?" and "How do we make that happen?" There are three pillars of a healthy life—sleep, nutrition, and exercise or movement. Each supports a physically healthy life and every dimension of our wellness and well-being. Improving one can help people live a better life. All three interact with and influence each other in multiple ways, and a three-pronged approach to improving all three may be a better way to improve physical, mental, and emotional health. Developing healthy habits within these three pillars is an important part of understanding that the more lifestyle behaviors we improve, the better our nervous system can function and the more likelihood there is of well-being. What follows is a discussion of the importance of these three pillars and recommendations to assist you in developing better sleep, nutrition, and exercise habits.

Sleep

Sleep deficiency includes sleep deprivation (i.e., when we do not get enough sleep), when we sleep at the wrong time of day, do not sleep well, do not get all the types of sleep the body needs, or if there is a sleep disorder that causes poor-quality sleep, such as sleep apnea (National Heart, Blood, and Lung Institute 2022). The National Sleep Foundation (2020) recommends that adults need between seven and nine hours' sleep every 24 hours. Children aged 6–12 need nine to 12 hours, and teenagers (i.e., aged 13–18) need eight to ten hours daily (Sleep Foundation 2022).

So many of us are sleep deprived, and our modern world isn't exactly friendly to us getting the right amount of sleep. Phone and tablet screens emit a blue light that impacts our sleep. Light pollution can impact our circadian rhythms, the natural sleep-wake cycles for humans. Many processed foods we eat disrupt our sleep patterns by impacting our bodies, and the sugar, fat, and salt mixture in many ultra-processed foods can energize us when we need to get some sleep (American Academy of Sleep Medicine 2016). Matthew Walker, author of the book *Why We Sleep: Unlocking the Power of Sleep and Dreams*, states, "More than a third of adults in many developed nations fail to obtain the recommended seven to nine hours of nightly sleep" (Walker 2017, p.1). For educators, sleep deprivation has almost been glorified as a part of our job. We get up early to make it to school before students arrive, and often stay up late creating lesson plans, reading student work, or grading exams. Overall, education systems in many parts of the world promote the idea that it is normal to be exhausted. It is almost seen as a badge of honor! We are supposed to be tired and stressed. We have normalized this as part of school culture, which is toxic for our bodies. Sleep deficiency among educators leads to burnout (Arvidsson *et al.* 2016; Bauer *et al.* 2006).

Even our start and end times for school are counter to our students' biology. Walker (2017) notes in his book:

Our children didn't always go to school at this biologically unreasonable time. A century ago, schools in the [United States] started at nine a.m. As a result, 95 percent of all children woke up without an alarm clock. Now, the inverse is true, caused by incessant marching back of school start times—which are in direct conflict with children's evolutionary preprogrammed need to be asleep during these precious, REM-sleep-rich morning hours. (p.310)

Walker (2017, p.310) notes that a study in Japan of more than 5000 schoolchildren showed that children with later start times also did better academically. One study of more than 11,500 students in the UK, aged 13–14, showed that sleep deficiency and sleep times are associated with hyperactivity and inattention and a higher risk of emotional and behavioral difficulties, with the manifestation of these difficulties showing externally in males and internally in females (Qiu & Morales-Muñoz 2022).

Sleep is not the absence of wakefulness. Sleep is when the body and brain engage in activities necessary to live and closely linked to our overall quality of life. While it may not appear as such during sleep, the whole body, including the brain, is very active, carrying out many functions related to our physical, emotional, and mental health—fundamental and sometimes highly complicated tasks that can only be achieved when we are not around to interfere. According to Walker (2017), we have two sleep stages—non-rapid eye movement sleep (called NREM sleep) and rapid eye movement sleep (called REM sleep). NREM and REM sleep occur during sleep cycles; an average sleep cycle lasts about 90 minutes. Ideally, we need four to six sleep cycles every 24 hours to feel fresh and rested. Our brain's electrical activity during these stages and cycles is busy clearing waste products, repairing tissues, building new bone tissue and muscle, strengthening our immune system, and helping to store, consolidate, and organize our memories (essential to learning). Sleep is essential to health. Poor sleep quality impacts nearly every system in the body, creating wide-ranging effects on the cardiovascular, endocrine, immune, and nervous systems (Singh, Yadav, & Jain 2019). Common health problems associated with poor sleep include diabetes, heart disease, obesity, stroke, and an increased risk of accidents (Institute of Medicine 2006). Sleep disruption further contributes to major mental health conditions, including depression, anxiety, and suicide (Walker 2017, p.1). This is indeed scary. This is why we call it restorative sleep—our bodies are restored. While science has yet to answer why we need sleep, it is clear that our brains and bodies need the time to do these important tasks.

This is a good place to acknowledge that this part of the journey highlights the divide between what we can change personally and what we can change at a system level. Our start times are unlikely to change anytime soon, yet individually, we can make changes to our own lives to try to increase the amount of rest we get. Now, if you are reading this as a person in a position of school leadership, here is where your professional and social justice journey intersects, and you are in a position to make important changes for children regarding the start and end of school times. Address the issues of sleep and rest in developing brains! Some of our students' life circumstances at home result in serious sleep deprivation. Surely, we need not punish young people for falling asleep at their desks. Is there a quiet space or room where they might take a nap?

Keep in mind that this is about regulation. If we can't find a reason to prioritize seven to nine hours of sleep a night, do it for our students! Remember that to share our regulated nervous system with them, we must have it to share. A lack of sleep is a deficit in our body budget. It equals dysregulation in our systems. We won't be able to be regulated educators if we are struggling with low energy from a lack of sleep.

So, we ask, "How much sleep do we need?" In Douglas Adams' book *The Hitchhiker's Guide to the Galaxy* (2017, first published 1979), the answer "of life, the Universe, and everything" is "forty-two" (pp.180–181). At least when it comes to sleep, that is the correct answer, according to science! We need to sleep about 42 percent of our lives—and we are just not doing it (Nagoski & Nagoski 2020).

Nutrition

A healthy dietary pattern includes understanding the difference between diet and nutrition. These terms are often used interchangeably, but their meanings differ. The term "diet" refers to the food we consume, whereas nutrition refers to the purpose of the food we eat for our body to function optimally (e.g., energy needs, tissue repair, and growth) to maintain good health. Nutritional balance from different food groups is the key to maintaining the body's budget critical to our health and well-being—focus on vegetables, fruit, whole grains, and low-fat proteins, and limit saturated fats, sodium, and sugar.

One of the main problems of prolonged chronic and traumatic stress is the depletion of nutrients. We need a healthy eating pattern to help regulate the nervous system. Prolonged and traumatic stress results in a long-term drain on our body's nervous system, requiring a lot of energy (i.e., calories), and utilizes much of our nutrient intake to produce and manufacture neurotransmitters like dopamine and serotonin. Serotonin plays an important role in mood regulation, and dopamine is involved in reward, motivation, and drive. Many whole and minimally processed foods are a natural source of these neurotransmitters or provide the ingredients necessary to manufacture these and many other neurotransmitters (Briguglio *et al.* 2018). Ellen Vora (2022), in her book *The Anatomy of Anxiety: Understanding and Overcoming the Body's Fear Response*, writes:

...the gut is home to our enteric nervous system, increasingly referred to as "the second brain," which produces, uses, and modulates more than thirty neurotransmitters...this second brain creates and stores 95 percent of the serotonin in our bodies, whereas only 5 percent of our serotonin is found in the brain. (p.23)

When we eat a well-balanced, nutritionally dense diet, especially of complex, minimally processed carbohydrates, our gut has the ingredients necessary for serotonin production. Serotonin helps us to feel good; if we want it to do its job, we must give it what it needs.

A well-balanced diet containing foods high in B vitamins is also important to our nervous system's functioning. Gregory Scott Brown (2022), in his book *The Self-Healing Mind: An Essential Five-Step Practice for Overcoming Anxiety and Depression, and Revitalizing Your Life*, writes about the importance of B vitamins and stress:

B vitamins, particularly vitamins B_6, B_{12}, and folate, are nutrients that play a useful role in brain development as well as aid in the production of neurotransmitters (like serotonin and dopamine) that help regulate mood. These vitamins also help build myelin, the fatty "insulation" that allows brain cells and circuits to communicate with each other more efficiently. When your diet doesn't have enough B vitamins, the brain suffers. To protect your mental health, you want to be sure you are incorporating some foods with these nutrients at every meal. You can find B vitamins in leafy greens, whole grains, pork, mussels, and eggs. (p.214)

No one food contains all the nutrients our brains and bodies require for optimal nervous system functioning, stressing the need for variety. Nutritional deficiencies play a significant role in our ability to remain regulated, affecting our mental and emotional health and our ability to *show up* as regulated adults in the classroom. We cannot achieve these things with unbalanced nutrition. Eating a variety of clean, whole, unprocessed foods is important because they provide natural sources of substances that exert crucial effects on the health of our nervous systems. Most calories in Western diets come from ultra-processed foods, and we should cut back on these. In Western culture, we tend to eat foods that fill us up but are scarce in nutrients. Highly processed foods mixed with sugars, fats, and high levels of salt can lead to nervous system dysregulation. These foods can also increase inflammation and kill off helpful gut bacteria (Shi 2019). When our brains experience and register a deficit in the body budget, our bodies will be out of balance.

Having established that eating fewer nutrient-dense foods compromises our metabolic needs, this is a good place to introduce the four categories of "foods according to the extent and purpose of food processing, rather than in terms of nutrients" (Monteiro *et al.* 2016) to help us to make better nutritional choices.

- *Unprocessed foods:* These foods are in their most natural state and have had no (or very minimal) processing. Examples include fruits and vegetables; whole grains, legumes, and nuts; meat, poultry, seafood, eggs, and milk; and herbs and spices. These foods should form the basis of your diet. A typical proportion of a meal on a healthy eating plate would contain about half vegetables and fruits, a quarter whole grains, and a quarter protein (Harvard University 2011). Translations of Harvard University's *Healthy Eating Plate* are available in over 25 languages.

- *Minimally processed foods:* These include the foods listed above but altered by the removal of inedible or unwanted parts by drying, crushing, or grinding; boiling, pasteurization, roasting, refrigeration, and freezing; and storage methods, such as placing in containers and vacuum packaging. Minimally processed foods do not contain added substances such as salt, sugar, oils, or fats. Serving sizes are similar to those listed for unprocessed foods.

- *Processed foods:* These include minimally processed foods as described above, but during processing, they are modified to increase their durability or enhance their sensory qualities (e.g., sight, taste, smell). These are common foods that have been altered, but not in a way that's detrimental to our health, although we want to be mindful of the added ingredients like salt, sugar, and nitrates, such as those found in processed meats. Food items include bread, cheese, and tofu; canned, salted, smoked, or cured meats, poultry, and seafood; canned fruits and vegetables; and legumes.

- *Ultra-processed foods:* These are foods that go through multiple processes (e.g., extrusion, molding, milling) and contain many added ingredients (e.g., coloring, added flavors, non-sugar sweeteners, and processing aids such as carbonation, anti-caking, and emulsifiers). Ultra-processed foods are cheap, convenient, and tasty, but too much consumption leads to becoming overweight or obese, heart disease, high blood pressure, and diabetes.

Eating mostly unprocessed or minimally processed foods will benefit nervous system regulation most. Lost nutrients during processing may be added back into the final product, but sometimes at a cost. The Nutrition Source at Harvard University (2023) writes:

> Depending on the degree of processing, nutrients can be destroyed or removed. Peeling outer layers of fruits, vegetables, and whole grains may remove plant nutrients (phytochemicals) and fiber. Heating or drying foods can destroy certain vitamins and minerals. Although food manufacturers can add back some of the nutrients lost, it is impossible to recreate the food in its original form.

For many, however, food is often an external means of internal regulation to control stress (e.g., stress eating). The irony of stress is that while we need more nutritionally dense food when exposed to high stress, we will often choose foods higher in fats and sugars (who doesn't love chocolate when stressed?), not only because of increased hunger but also because of their comfort factor. Some of this stress eating may be attributed to our body's prediction systems and what might be needed to cope energy-wise; that is, in times of stress, our brains can crave high-calorie foods for energy and because stress hormones like cortisol and ghrelin can increase hunger (Sominsky & Spencer 2014)—so there is no fault here, as part of this craving is a biological process. Nonetheless, we tend to crave certain foods under stressful conditions (e.g., fat, sugar, salt) because they make us feel better—sometimes we eat to soothe ourselves (to feel regulated), at least temporarily because they boost our brain's "happy" chemicals, like serotonin and dopamine. At first glance, that sounds like a good thing. We eat some ice cream, get a dopamine hit, and "boom," we feel satisfied (i.e., regulated). The body budget gets balanced in the short term. It gets a little more complicated in the long term as the earlier surplus creates a later deficit (like a sugar crash) that may become problematic.

In this section about nutrition, we understand that planning and sticking to a balanced nutritional program is challenging, especially when we are busy and stressed. Sometimes, stress causes us to be too busy to eat properly, or to skip meals or forget to eat (Gonzalez & Miranda-Massari 2014). We are not writing recipes or providing state-of-the-art nutritional advice but rather providing the link between eating, nervous system regulation, and regulating the body's budget. A holistic approach to diet and nutrition involves reflecting on what matters to us and what the underlying motivators of our eating habits are. Unhealthy eating patterns will only result in an increased level of stress, followed by health problems in the future, without effective stress management. Think about what we crave when we are stressed. How does it measure up in terms of meeting our nutritional needs? We can build a good diet by understanding which foods offer what nutrients and what influences our eating patterns. The message is clear—we need to be on top of our food game, or it will be on top of us!

Movement and exercise

In Chapter 4, we learned that a bottom-up strategy to keep us regulated involves rhythmic, patterned, and repetitive activity. In this section, we discuss the interconnectedness of the brain and body, emphasizing the importance of regular physical activity for developing and supporting the health of our nervous system.

Earlier in this chapter, we mentioned that the *stress response* happens in the body as it prepares to manage a stressor's challenges. The body will automatically respond to prepare itself for *fight or flight*, as there is no initial conscious control. Our heart and respiratory rate increases, and our muscles receive more blood. All types of stress (e.g., acute, acute episodic, chronic) can make us feel on high alert. This can be stress from a job, home life, or caring for another. The problem is that this stress has nowhere to go. It gets pent up in our bodies unless we release it. Exercise can allow your body to release this excess energy. Exercise and movement have been shown to help close the stress cycle by aiding our body to expel excess stress hormones like cortisol and burning up the excess energy stress brings. Emily and Amelia Nagoski write, "Physical activity is the single most efficient strategy for completing the stress response cycle...literally any movement of your body—is your first line of attack in the battle against burnout" (2020, p.5). Movement helps to regulate our body's budget.

Let's step aside for a moment and talk about exercise. We can also call it physical activity, movement, a workout, training, strength training, or sport—choose what makes you feel most comfortable when talking about it. We realize that exercise is not everyone's game! Our affinity for exercise falls on a continuum—not everyone likes to do it, others love it, and most fall somewhere in between. The terms we listed above are planned and structured activities and programs designed exclusively for moving our bodies. There are other ways we move our bodies daily that are not necessarily planned or structured. We can refer to this type of physical activity as non-exercise activity thermogenesis (NEAT) (Comana 2022). NEAT includes all the physical activity we do throughout the day that is not part of a planned and structured physical exercise program or when we are asleep or eating. It can include the energy expended to get ready for work. Do you stand all day at work, or are you taking many steps? Do you do your housework and yardwork or hire someone to help? Do you cook or eat out? Do you do most of your shopping in person or online? Mental and cognitive tasks, like reading and writing, also burn energy. Are you a fidgeter? Activities like these increase our non-resting energy needs. Even small activities can increase our metabolic rate. Not everyone has the time for planned, structured exercise programs, yet if we rethink where and how we are burning energy, what is important is that we get our bodies moving.

Regular, planned physical activity creates stress in our bodies, but this is good stress. When physical activity is planned and repeated, the stress response is how our body's systems adapt to and overcome the stress associated with movement if the movement is progressive and created to fit individual needs and helps us to reach our personal goals. When we engage in a sustainable physical activity program that fits our unique interests and abilities, the stress we place on our bodies leads to an adaptive stress response. Our muscle cells' adaptation to exercise improves, as do other cells and tissues in our body, like those in our brain and the rest of our nervous system. Recall that neuroplasticity is the ability of our brain to rewire itself in response to learning and experience. Adult neurogenesis is the ability to grow new neurons (i.e., brain cells). Physical exercise promotes both, improving brain function, especially in the hippocampus (de Sousa *et al.* 2020), the structure in the limbic area of our brain that is responsible for indexing memories for storage and recall. Like the stress patterns we use to build resilience, our adaptation to exercise must be moderate, controllable, and predictable (see "Resilience, dosing, and spacing" in Chapter 6). For our bodies to adapt to the benefits of physical activity and exercise, it must also be regular and progressive. When we do that, we increase our body's ability to accurately predict what we need to live better, not only with exercise but in many other areas of life. We cannot build these benefits with on-and-off approaches to exercise.

Any planned physical activity is a way to improve skills that can enhance our inhibitory control. As we plan and learn a new activity, we challenge our nervous system to become more effective at performing and responding to that activity and our brain's ability to predict. There is also some cross-over in our ability to control our impulses (like having that second piece of chocolate) and choosing behaviors that align with our values and beliefs—how we want to live our lives! Self-control is a very important part of stress management; it is also important in choosing which behaviors to do and which we should not do. At that moment, when we feel our nervous system becoming dysregulated (i.e., stressed), the training our nervous system experiences due to our regular physical activity also allows us to tap into our cortex and decide how to respond to the stressor. This, too, takes training, and exercise allows that to happen.

We are about to move on and discuss the importance of relational health. However, we might ask, "Which is more important—sleep, nutrition, or exercise?" They are so intertwined that one is no more important than the other. What we eat can either fuel or thwart our workout. Regular physical activity can benefit our sleep, but what we eat (e.g., ultra-processed foods and caffeine) can decrease sleep quality. When we do not get enough sleep, we overeat and crave unhealthy foods. Sleep offers our bodies time to renew and restore, but our exercise can suffer if our muscles are not well rested and restored. Sleep underpins diet and exercise. Most people can function if hungry or they do not move their bodies much, but few can function without adequate rest. Whichever choice we make about where to start in changing our behavior, we want to begin by taking baby steps toward our goals, as this allows our brain and nervous system to adapt to change gradually so that they do not feel threatened. For example, cutting too many calories at once or exerting ourselves on a new exercise program might help us to feel proud of our efforts. Still, our brain and nervous system may feel threatened, which can stifle our progress; they need time to adapt. We want to be mindful of our body budget and how our body (and nervous system) feels if we did not sleep well last night, skipped breakfast or lunch today, or have too much pent-up energy racing in our body because of a stressful day.

RELATIONAL HEALTH

Restorative work and trauma-informed work are both humanistic and relational approaches. For more than a thousand years, hunter-gatherer communities and Indigenous peoples across the globe knew the importance of robust, healthy relationships for survival. Much of today's global movements for restorative justice are rooted in indigenous philosophies of community and relationship.

As humans and mammals, we are social herd creatures wired for attachment. Sadly, our modern world puts many infants and small children in a precarious situation where they are forced to choose between attachment and authenticity (Maté & Maté 2022). Can I get my irreducible needs for attachment, love, care, and survival met and still be who I am in my heart? That is a profoundly risky position to place a child in whose brain is not fully developed—pitting two basic human needs against each other.

Bruce Alexander, an American psychologist, did a set of amazing experiments in the 1970s on rats that demonstrated how social creatures like most mammals, including humans, are wired for and drawn to connection and socialization (Alexander et al. 1981). The experiments also showed a glimmer of the pain social isolation can cause social creatures. Isolated rats were placed in a cage with two water bottles, one filled with plain water and the other with either heroin or cocaine water. The rats would drink from the drug water repeatedly until they eventually overdosed. Alexander was curious if the drugs were the cause of the overdoses or if the environment they were in caused this sad demise, so he changed it up and tried a variation. He put the rats in "rat parks" with other rats. They were permitted to run free, socialize, have sex, eat when they wanted, and play. Again, there were two water bottles, one filled with plain water and one with drugs, except the rats hardly touched the drugs this time. Even if they did take a few "hits" of the drugs, it was in moderation without overdosing. In response to the current opioid epidemic, Sederer (2019) writes, "Humans, not just rats, need to be part of a community, encouraged to relate and experience the support of others." This demonstrates not only the importance of relationships and community but also how environments influence behavior. Sometimes, we expect children to change when the environment, circumstances, and conditions need to change. Perhaps we need to consider our isolation/seclusion policies in our schools—the use of detention and suspension: purposeful isolation as punishment—when what is really needed is reconnection and reintegration into the school herd.

Currently, Western culture is hyper-individualistic. Rather than living in multi-generational and multi-family homes where a child will have multiple caregivers, we celebrate the idea of mom, dad, and 2.5 children. Even our TV shows glorify the small settings where children have fewer and fewer caregivers, and the family unit is small. We celebrate single moms working multiple jobs as heroes while failing to acknowledge how cruel it is that our culture forces a child to have a single caregiver and a mom who is guaranteed not to be able to meet her own needs, let alone those of a child.

In her book *Hunt, Gather, Parent: What Ancient Cultures Can Teach Us About the Lost Art of Raising Happy, Helpful Little Humans*, Michaeleen Doucleff (2021) reminds us:

> If you look around the world—and investigate human history—you'll find that the nuclear family (and a mom whose sole job is parenting) is arguably one of the most nontraditional structures out there. For 99.9 percent of the time humans have been on earth, the nuclear

family simply didn't exist. "It's a family structure that has been around for a tiny pinprick in human history," says historian John Gillis, at Rutgers University, who has been studying the evolution of Western families for more than thirty years. "It isn't old. It isn't traditional. It doesn't have any real roots in the past." (p.25)

We are living in a culture that is biologically and socially out of sync with our human evolution. Our brains are not designed to live like this. We are designed to live in communities with strong social support systems. Our modern world is suffering from relational poverty, as Dr. Bruce Perry (Perry & Winfrey 2021) writes:

Simply put, modern life provides fewer opportunities for relational interactions. In a multifamily, multigenerational environment, the continuous social interactions provide a rich source of regulation, reward, and learning. And that's how we used to live. In 1790, 63 percent of our nation's households had five or more people; only 10 percent had two or fewer. Today those numbers have basically flipped: in 2006, only 8 percent of households had five or more people; 60 percent had two or fewer. In a recent survey of selected urban communities in the U.S., Europe, and Japan, up to 60 percent of all households were just one person. (pp.258–259)

Too many demands are placed on parents, particularly single parents, because we live these disconnected, isolated lives. There are insufficient social resources to meet our or our children's needs.

In 2023, the United States Surgeon General posted an advisory document attempting to curb the epidemic of loneliness and isolation (Office of the US Surgeon General 2023). The report outlines the health consequences of a society not designed for social connectedness and encourages citizens to center social connectedness in policies, programs, schools, and places of employment. The advisory states:

Loneliness is far more than just a bad feeling—it harms both individual and societal health. It is associated with a greater risk of cardiovascular disease, dementia, stroke, depression, anxiety, and premature death. The mortality impact of being socially disconnected is similar to that caused by smoking up to 15 cigarettes a day, and even greater than that associated with obesity and physical inactivity. And the harmful consequences of a society that lacks social connection can be felt in our schools, workplaces, and civic organizations, where performance, productivity, and engagement are diminished. (p.4)

What does this mean for our wellness? Dr. Bruce Perry (Perry & Winfrey 2021, p.108) writes, "Our major finding is that your history of relational health—your connectedness to family, community, and culture—is more predictive of your mental health than your history of adversity." Instead of telling children to work hard to succeed, we would do much better for our children if we taught them that their success is more dependent on the support systems they build. Instill the value of kinship and connection and that everyone has value, gifts to offer, and worth, even if one may not be experiencing that right now at the moment where you are.

MINDFULNESS
Over the last decade or more, mindfulness has become a trendy word, conjuring up all sorts of ideas from studies by top neuroscientists to self-help gurus. In education, mindfulness is both a skill and a practice (Brummer & Thorsborne 2020). When educators can stay grounded in stressful moments, it is as if that contagious state of calm can be shared with students in distress.

Mindfulness is a technique for slowing down enough to experience our emotions and feelings to help us develop our thoughts clearly. It can be a valuable tool for those who want to master self-regulation of our bodies, including our emotions. Mindfulness offers us tools to do just that. The elements of mindfulness, namely awareness and non-judgmental acceptance of one's moment-to-moment experience, are regarded as potentially effective antidotes to the maladaptive processes that inhibit, rather than support, wellness-enhancing behavior (Bishop *et al.* 2004). Mindfulness, as part of the "Five Skills of Restorative," is also discussed in Chapter 7.

We learn through mindfulness practice that emotions and feelings are data that do not define who we are but are essential in helping us regulate our behavior. Barrett (2017) writes that emotions help us to make meaning, help us to prescribe action, and help us to regulate our body budget (pp.138–139). Mindfulness practices teach us to listen to ourselves. It is a process of regulating our attention to the awareness of our everyday experiences and relating our thoughts and emotions to those experiences with curiosity and openness. When we stay mindful and aware of our body's sensations and interoception, we can better regulate our emotional states because we become aware of the context where these emotions arise. That gnawing in our gut could be hunger, nervousness, or maybe we caught the flu. When present in these moments, we can witness these sensations with a mindset of curiosity rather than cognitively trying to label the feeling.

I (Marg) know that when I'm in a hurry to get somewhere, and I have miscalculated traffic congestion and am running late, I worry about not showing up on time, being unreliable—the whole cascade of thoughts we are familiar with, mostly focusing on beating myself up. I become aware that I am panting! If I'm lucky, I remember to do the mindful thing—to be a witness to my thoughts instead of arguing with them and just being curious. I take a few deep breaths. This all helps me turn up in a better state of mind—regulated!

FINAL THOUGHTS

This book, as emphasized in this chapter, is a call to action to revisit self-care and wellness. Self-care must also become community care as we are so interconnected that our choices, actions, and the cultures we create impact all of us. Barrett (2017) sums it up in this simple paragraph:

Modern culture, unfortunately, is engineered to screw up your body budget. Many of the products sold in supermarkets and chain restaurants are pseudo-food loaded with budget-warping refined sugar and bad fats. Schools and jobs require you to wake early and go to sleep late, leaving over 40 percent of Americans between the ages of thirteen and sixty-four regularly sleep deprived, a condition that can lead to chronic misbudgeting and possibly depression and other mental illnesses. Advertisers play on your insecurities, suggesting you'll be judged badly by your friends unless you buy the right clothing or car, and social rejection is toxic for your body budget. Social media offers new opportunities for social rejection and adds ambiguity, which is even worse for your body budget. Friends and employers expect you to be surgically attached to your cell phone at all hours, which means you never truly relax, and late-night screen time disrupts your sleeping patterns. Your culture's expectations for work, rest, and socializing determine how easily you can manage that internal budget. Social reality transmutes into physical reality. (p.177)

CENTRAL IDEAS

★ Wellness and well-being are reciprocal and evolve throughout our lives. Our well-being is a positive orientation of our overall being, and our wellness activities are the many paths we use to get there. Our wellness activities support our well-being. We want to be mindful of our processes, patterns, and activities supporting our well-being.

★ Using prediction as a guide, our brain's number-one job is maintaining and managing the body's budget and ensuring that the right quantities of our body's resources are directed where they are needed at any given time. When we are not regulated, our prediction systems can malfunction, making prediction errors about the world around us.

★ Stress is our response to a stressor. Stress often shows up as a symptom of disease. We may not always be able to avoid the stressor, yet we can work to manage the stress cycle. Our stress is a cycle that needs to be completed and dealt with to keep us healthy.

★ A well-regulated nervous system helps us to navigate stressors in our world more easily. When we are dysregulated, our systems do not perform as well, and that stress can impact our work with students.

★ We have three main pillars of wellness (sleep, nutrition, and exercise) and a few other areas that need to be kept on our radar (mindfulness, relational health, and our use of technology).

★ Each of us is unique and the expert of our own lives. Each of us is responsible for discovering our real needs and finding ways to meet them. Our approach requires self-knowledge and mental and emotional flexibility to make the best choices for our health and well-being.

★ Our human evolution dictates that we are designed to live in communities with strong support systems. Every individual has worth, provides value, and has gifts to offer.

★ Practicing mindfulness supports our well-being by allowing us to develop self-regulation as we slow down to experience our emotions and feelings in the present moment without evaluation or judgment.

REFLECTION QUESTIONS

✓ In each of the various dimensions of wellness (e.g., physical, mental, emotional, relational, intellectual, spiritual, and vocational), describe your awareness of your processes, patterns, and activities that support your overall well-being.

✓ Sleep, nutrition, and exercise are three pillars of a healthy life that support better nervous system regulation. Considering these pillars, what are the processes, patterns, and activities you engage in that support or hinder this process?

✓ Our human evolution dictates that we are designed to live in communities. Reflect on your history of relational health, the present, and your connectedness to family, community, and culture. How in sync are you with creating and nourishing relationships with others regarding our evolutionary heritage? How do you honor your uniquenesses and enjoy the uniquenesses of others and the gifts you and others bring that support our evolutionary roots of social connectedness?

✓ Realizing your connectedness to all things—physical and social—describe the processes, patterns, and activities in a way that is congruent with (e.g., supports) that awareness. Where can you improve in creating and nourishing relationships with others?

✓ Mindful practices teach us to listen to ourselves. How do you use your mind and thoughts to support, not hinder, your wellness activities and overall well-being? How aware are you of recurring thoughts that occupy your mind throughout the day, and if these are life-affirming? How aware are you of the connection between your thoughts and emotions?

In our next chapter, Trauma, Adversity, and a Regulated Classroom, we explore a little more about trauma, how we currently live in our world, and how school can play a role in mitigating this trauma or intensifying it, especially when we are working with older ways of interpreting behavior. We offer some practical advice to improve regulation in the classroom, including Dr. Bruce Perry's six Rs approach to the curriculum: relevant, rewarding, rhythmic, repetitious, relational, and respectful.

— CHAPTER 6 —

Trauma, Adversity, and a Regulated Classroom

Now that we have a better idea about the basics of brain development, structure, and function (Chapter 3) and regulation (Chapter 4), in this chapter, we take a closer look at the impacts of trauma, adversity, and neglect and how they impact the brain and body, and the implications for this in our classrooms. Here is an interesting analogy from Dr. Lori Desautels (2023) to remind us how our past experiences act as a filter for our present experiences:

> Our nervous systems are as unique as thumbprints. Each of us carries around an individualized backpack that holds our distinctive perceptual maps of the world. Those maps have been unconsciously created to help us interpret and survive, as we are constantly detecting the "temperature" of a safe or threatening environment, relationship, or experience. (p.25)

Our own world experiences influence how we perceive a student's behavior. We bring our backpack of experiences and perceptual maps into our classrooms, and we see everything that happens in that classroom through those maps, influencing how we respond. That includes our biases and prejudices about people, our cues of safety or danger in the environment, and even our curiosity.

PREDICTION AND THE TRAUMATIZED BRAIN

Chapter 3 explored the issue of the brain's capacity to predict. As a reminder, our brain is a meaning-making machine using the information from our five senses and our interoceptive systems to help us predict what will happen next. We live then in a state of predictability or anticipation (Barrett 2017). Our brain uses the information from the outside and inside worlds, comparing it to our previous experiences to anticipate what might happen. It prepares itself by predicting what will happen next. *Unfortunately, trauma can distort this prediction system with "false" predictions.* Traditional discipline systems built on carrots and sticks (behaviorism) often fail to deliver the results we expect because this approach is misguided about the causes of behavior—we have no idea how the child's brain is predicting because their brain is unique to their own experiences and has developed to improve their chances of survival.

We use a stimulus-response mental model in our old-school way of thinking about human behavior. It is a model that assumes the brain is dormant, waiting for a stimulus to cause a reaction. This is the antecedent-behavior-consequence approach to behavior commonly underpinning our functional behavioral assessments. This view can be more than misleading. We may think a child is reacting to being told "no" (by having a tantrum or being defiant) or being asked to do a challenging task (refusing to do it or walking away). In reality, that might be only half the story. The brain uses the current sensory information and compares it to all its past experiences to determine the meaning of the current experience so it can prepare what it needs to do next. For most of our children, it is unlikely that their underdeveloped and immature brains can manipulate the world around them. While *we* may describe the behavior as "manipulative," being able to manipulate is a highly cognitive, mature skill, and it would be better for us to be curious about what might be going on for them rather than making such assumptions. If their past experiences are overwhelming or scary, they see the present moment through that scary lens and may predict that even benign events are threatening. They will then prepare for what they believe is about to happen, possibly believing they are in danger even when they are not.

Trauma is a normal response to an abnormal situation out of our control. What may be traumatic for one person may not be traumatizing for someone else. That is due to the uniqueness of each of our nervous systems. Every moment we experience is filtered through our backpack of past experiences. If our past is filled with experiences that lead us to believe the world is unsafe, that people are scary, or that hope is dim, we will likely experience the world through that lens. For some of us, trauma was the neglect, unavailability, or inconsistency of caregivers. It goes beyond just what happened. It was also *what didn't happen* that was needed developmentally.

A helpful way to understand this concept of what is and what isn't traumatic is provided by the United States government's Substance Abuse and Mental Health Services Administration (2014) and its three Es Framework: The *Event*, the *Experience*, and the *Effects*. Two people can have the same event happen to them and have unique experiences and effects. Trauma happens when our nervous systems become overloaded and overwhelmed by the events; circumstances, and emotions around us to a point where we cannot cope. These experiences become amplified when no caring, attuned adult can buffer the impacts and offer a sense of felt safety. It is not enough to recognize these events or experiences as traumatic. We also need to be aware of the relational supports a child has or doesn't have. These events and experiences may not be capital "T" traumas but never-ending circumstances that engage our threat response systems. Little "t" traumas can be the constant microaggressions students feel when they are different or bullied. This is covered again in Chapter 8, where we link trauma and shame.

Policies, practices, and systems that cause trauma have become normalized. We no longer realize how pervasive these impacts are. In many cultures, trauma survivors don't even know they are experiencing trauma because it is simply "normal" or culturally acceptable for them. Corporal punishment in families and schools in the United States and other countries is a good example of a normalized practice that causes trauma. It has become so common that some believe children actually "need" to be hit, spanked, or paddled. It is the same with a chaotic home life, abuse, violence, and neglect. These examples are experiences that are just a "part of life" and how everyone is treated. We must realize that our brains and bodies are not wired to thrive with this treatment, which will impact our body budget.

In the book *The Myth of Normal: Trauma, Illness & Healing in a Toxic Culture*, Dr. Gabor Maté (Maté & Maté 2022) writes:

> I will make the case that much of what passes for normal in our society is neither healthy nor natural, and that to meet modern society's

criteria for normality is, in many ways, to conform to requirements that are profoundly abnormal in regard to our Nature-given needs—which is to say, unhealthy and harmful on the physiological, mental, and even spiritual levels. (pp.7–8)

The road to trauma-informed thinking requires us to see past this curtain of toxicity we call normal to create safer circumstances for our students to learn and for our educators to work. To do this, we must know how the nervous system works, starting with our own. We must identify the blind spots where toxicity passes for normality. We must change our responses to children's behavior from punitive, angry, or passive-aggressive to co-regulation and skill-building.

In our Western culture today, many developmental milestones are being thwarted by our modern world. We see parents handing a child a smartphone to distract them rather than "serve and return," the process by which parents and child make matching faces, smiling and giggling at each other. While this seems like a small thing, developmentally this is an important function we humans have engaged in as part of our evolution for thousands of years. We see families out to dinner, and instead of engaging in genuine, mutually interesting, intrinsically rewarding conversations, the children and their caregivers stare at their screens. We are paying the price for this. Our technology is developing faster than our brains can adapt. We are also neglecting our social need to be relationally connected and to develop the skills to do this. At this point, we do not yet know the long-term impact of this on the developing brain.

Our schools also contribute to this toxic culture as young minds are force-fed lessons driven by a curriculum specialist (mandated curriculum and testing), not human curiosity. Our students are being forced to sit for hours when they are at an age when they should be moving, exploring, and building relational problem-solving skills with each other. When students' bodies resist this sitting for hours, we punish them or drug them, believing they have attention deficits or disorders rather than considering how we teach, which is completely out of sync with our brain's evolution over the last 200,000 years.

For thousands of years, children were raised in hunter-gatherer societies using time-tested parenting techniques based on a child's irreducible needs (Maté & Maté 2022). In some cases, our current cultures have done a complete 180-degree turn on these approaches, and the results are devastating. It's no question that today's youth are facing an urgent mental health crisis. For example:

- After a two-year decline in 2019 and 2020, suicide rates among youth in the United States increased in 2021, according to the United States Centers for Disease Control and Prevention (Stone, Mack, & Qualters 2023).

- Adolescents' reports of anxiety, stress, and mental health challenges are increasing. A study released by the U.S. Department of Health and Human Services in 2022 found that between 2016 and 2020, the number of children aged 3 to 17 diagnosed with anxiety grew by 29 percent and those diagnosed with depression grew by 27 percent (Lebrun-Harris *et al.* 2022).

- Similar increases in anxiety, stress, and mental health challenges in young people, including worrying and feeling less safe at school, were found in findings from the *Mission Australia Youth Survey 2022* (Mission Australia 2022, p.8) and the *Mental Health of Children and Young People in England 2022—Wave 3 Follow up to the 2017 Survey in England* (Health and Social Care Information Centre 2022).

"Trauma-informed" has become somewhat of a buzzword in education. Unhappily, many of us do not yet fully understand the connection between trauma and the impacts it has on a student's ability to learn (cognitive regulation), their ability to sit still (biological "physical" regulation), their ability to handle big emotions (emotional regulation), and how they manage social interactions and conflict resolution (social regulation). For educators, knowing how trauma impacts the brain holds the key to knowing how to help students succeed better in their education. As we wrote in our first book:

> Trauma is not the events we experience; it is our response to these events. It lives in our central nervous system as part of our stress response. In all respects it is a dysregulated nervous system. It is our response to events that surpass our nervous system's ability to cope with abuse, bullying, loss, neglect, pain, witnessing or experiencing

violence, and even systemic issues like homophobia, poverty, racism, or other forms of discrimination. (Brummer & Thorsborne 2020, p.48)

We have various nervous system states that can mix a range of our sympathetic (fight-flight-mobilized) and parasympathetic (freeze-faint-immobilized) systems to help us navigate the world. These states slide on a continuum from calm, alert, alarm, fear, and terror as part of the concept we wrote about in Chapter 3. This is referred to as "state-dependent brain functioning." As information from the outside and inside worlds enters the brainstem, it is compared to all the information our brains have stored in that region. The process is repeated for each layer or system, moving from the brainstem to the motor brain, the social/emotional brain, and the cortex, working sequentially from the bottom up. If anything cues up a threat response, our nervous system will change our "state" to help us prepare to function with the experience. When lower parts of the brain are aroused, higher brain regions will lose some of their ability to function. This means we can only access as much of our brain's functionality as our nervous system allows us in our current context. When stress/threat is high, access to higher brain functions like reasoning and reflection is low. When we are regulated, safe, and relational, our access to higher thinking, reflection, and reasoning is high. A key concept in this book is learning how to recognize our state and our students' states.

RESILIENCE, DOSING, AND SPACING

According to Dr. Bruce Perry's Neurosequential Model, stress can be our friend when it happens in predictable, controllable, and moderate patterns. This type of stress builds resilience. Examples might be experiences like failing an exam, temporary separation from a caregiver, or changing schools. When children experience these types of stress with relational buffers from adults, the results can be growth and resilience. This is often referred to as developmental stress.

Stress patterns must be moderate, controllable, and predictable to build resilience. When stress is unpredictable, prolonged, or uncontrollable, it is likely to sensitize a body to more easily be traumatized or re-traumatized (Perry & Winfrey 2021).

An example of this would be a child's day at school. When every day of a student's time in school is spent "in struggle," constantly being corrected, punished, and excluded from recess, lunch, or class due to their behavior, it will likely become a pattern of sensitizing stress. It is unpredictable because the student doesn't know when they will be called out or the intensity or severity of the punishment, and there are few rest periods between episodes. On the flip side of the coin, if a child comes to school and is given challenges that are predictable and moderate and choices have been offered to allow for control (as described in self-determination theory in Chapter 2), it is likely this student is going to build resilience to the demands of learning. Add some rest and recess to the mix, and we build resilience. When children come to school and are repeatedly reinforced with positive acknowledgment, genuinely listened to, and feel understood and supported in their efforts to achieve, their brains release dopamine, serotonin, and oxytocin (feel-good hormones). This will likely build positive outcomes for them.

The concept of dosing and spacing can mean that a big trauma experience that happens just once can be as impactful as repeated small microtraumas that are unpredictable, uncontrollable, and prolonged. Examples of microtraumas could be constant verbal abuse of a child or repeatedly dismissing their feelings as unimportant. What matters is the timing between and frequency of experiences (spacing), the intensity of an experience (dosing), and the relational buffers that help co-regulate the nervous system during these experiences.

For some of our students, there is little spacing between the little "t" traumas they experience. It is a daily constant stream of chaos, demand, lack of control, and emotional punches they need to navigate. Many of these little "t" traumas result from systemic issues like fighting, poverty, racism, and homophobia; others are personal issues like having to parent younger siblings, having alcoholic parents, lacking adult support, sexual abuse, verbal abuse, bullying, and other daily stressful issues. We should be grateful that they still turn up and engage in learning!

This idea of dosing and spacing also matters in our therapeutic approaches and behavior interventions. Humans, especially young ones, can only revisit the trauma they have experienced in small doses (Perry & Winfrey 2021), perhaps just seconds at a time. If we want to change behaviors children have developed as coping strategies, we must remember that the behavior is also laced with traumatic memories. It will take baby steps, repeated often with a trusted adult.

Hopefully, we can see now that trauma is an experience of our entire being (body and brain). It looks different in each person due to the uniqueness of our nervous systems. As educators, we can still see some common predictions surface. If a child in our classroom has a brain that predicts danger or threat, their body will prepare for a fight, a run, or a shutdown. It doesn't matter if it was a big "T" or a little "t" experience; it is still trauma. It doesn't matter if we are wealthy or poor. Trauma doesn't care. It is not a competition. No individual's trauma is worse or better than anyone else's, because it is unique to the person's experience. The lower parts of the brain don't evaluate trauma or compare it; they prepare us to stay safe in the future.

What can one person do? That is the magic question! We want educators to understand our impact on and power over the lives of developing children. What is a fleeting moment of our day can be a lifelong, impacting memory for a child. On April 26, 2023, actor, director, and writer Kevin Smith, known to many as "Silent Bob" from the movie *Clerks*, posted a video on YouTube titled *Trauma is Trauma: A Mental Health Talk with Kevin Smith* (Smith 2023). In his video, Smith tells the story of a fourth-grade teacher who made comments in disgust about his weight. He talks of how humiliating and painful that moment was, and at age 52, he was still healing from the pain it caused. While it was most likely a fleeting moment for that educator, it was not for fourth-grade Kevin. The age at which a child experiences pain or threat will greatly impact the effects those experiences can have. As adults, we are more likely to handle comments of this sort because our brains are more mature, perhaps even challenging disrespect or nastiness. Still, the capacity of a child to put such comments aside is negligible. These wounds can be profound and long-lasting.

Harvard University's National Scientific Council on the Developing Child (2015) released a paper that reminds us that children who do well despite serious hardship have had at least one stable and committed relationship with a supportive adult. It says:

Whether the burdens come from the hardships of poverty, the challenges of parental substance abuse or serious mental illness, the stresses of war, the threats of recurrent violence or chronic neglect, or a combination of factors, the single most common finding is that children who end up doing well have had at least one stable and committed relationship with a supportive parent, caregiver, or other adult. These relationships provide the personalized responsiveness, scaffolding, and protection that buffer children from developmental disruption. They also build key capacities—such as the ability to plan, monitor and regulate behavior, and adapt to changing circumstances—that enable children to respond to adversity and to thrive. This combination of supportive relationships, adaptive skill-building, and positive experiences constitutes the foundations of what is commonly called resilience. (p.1)

These relationships buffer children from developmental disruption and help them develop resilience, or the skills needed to respond to adversity and to thrive. We want to remind ourselves that we could be that one adult for a child who knocks them down or lifts them. How do we want to be remembered? How do we want to impact our students—with kindness or cruelty?

For me (Joe), it was Rosemary O'Conner, one of my fifth-grade teachers. She knew I was being bullied, and this was a day and age where bullying was seen as a rite of passage. Most adults did nothing to intervene, and the bullying was relentless throughout my middle school years. She went to great lengths to foster my musical talents, give me someone to talk to, and, more importantly, a place to hide from the bullies. She would let me play guitar with her for school activities. As I advanced into middle school, I would return to her classroom each day after school to hang out. She knew I was smoking cigarettes at a young age, yet she didn't seek to turn me in to the principal, Sr. Mary. She would talk with me about my smoking habit. She left doors open to let me speak and was a great listener. Her non-judgmental approach is what kept me coming back for more relational rewards. In high school, it was my music teacher, Florence Murtha. This wonderful human also knew I was a struggling child with a tough home life. She always made her classroom available to me when she wasn't in it. I could play piano and practice my singing every day, improving my ability to do what I wanted. I am forever grateful for her kindness and words; we are still in touch today.

REGULATE, RELATE, REASON AS CLASSROOM MANAGEMENT

Our classrooms need to be relational spaces, creating a strong sense of belonging and connection where every student feels seen, heard, and valued for the gifts they bring and is supported to manage their challenges. A regulated classroom will be one where students' basic needs for food, water, rest, and ample movement have all been met so their body budget is balanced—the heart of regulation. Only then are academics and other learning possible. We must bring this new lens into our classroom to become trauma-informed and restorative. Remember our advice from Chapter 4 that lists the ingredients for regulation: patterned, rhythmic, repetitive actions—students will need predictable routines. This means putting the engagement sequence into action—we are talking about *regulate, relate, reason.*

Regulate

Helping our students to be regulated starts with a regulated class-room. We need a regulated classroom with a healthy social climate where students feel as if they belong so we can reach the parts of the brain that allow for learning and academics. Students will need a sense of felt safety, even more so if they come from a history of adversity. In our first book, *Building a Trauma-Informed Restorative School: Skills and Approaches for Improving Culture and Behavior* (Brummer & Thorsborne 2020), on pages 56–69, we detail strategies for a regulated classroom. Here, we summarize these main points and add some new information.

Regulated and attuned educator

The first step to having a regulated classroom is having a regulated and attuned educator. The state of our nervous system is contagious, and when dysregulated, we risk dysregulating our students. We must ask ourselves, "What nervous system state am I sharing with my students?" and, "Am I even aware of my nervous system state?" We must work on minding our nervous system states and noticing the behaviors that students exhibit that trigger dysregulation in us. This might help us to refocus our energy away from viewing everything through a compliance lens and take the opportunity to teach children to regulate their nervous systems.

Sensory needs of students

Trauma can impact the sensory processing of children. That means our classrooms need to be mindful of sensory needs. Some children who have experienced trauma or are neurodivergent may become overly sensitive to different sensory overload, while others will crave it. It is important to watch children's responses to the environment and be mindful of when behaviors occur and what needs are trying to be met with the behavior. Sensory blocking or sensory seeking can lead to behavior issues. This will include smells, sounds, lights, chairs, how untidy a room is, and even the decoration in the room. Think of a spa. When you come into a spa, the lights have likely been turned down a bit; soft music and maybe a waterfall are making relaxing sounds. It is an intentional space focused on turning your nervous system down a few notches. We need that type of intention in our classroom. Remember that a child's brain takes in lots of new information about their physical surroundings if they are new to the classroom. Adults have more of a stored template of the world, whereas children take in lots of new information daily. This means everything for a child is new and novel and, therefore, can much more easily overwhelm a child's sensory systems. A cluttered or overwhelming amount of sensory information can dysregulate a child. What follows are some practical considerations about the physical appearance and design of the classroom.

- Keep the classroom as tidy and uncluttered as possible, as mess and clutter can be overstimulating. When organizing materials, use natural materials that children can touch and feel (Sorrells 2015).

- Consider the arrangement of seating and chairs and if these enhance collaboration and cooperation. Use flexible seating to accommodate different body types, including stability balls, chairs, and beanbags.

- Consider the color of the walls. Are they soothing (e.g., pastel blues, greens, yellows) or overly exciting (bright reds)?

- Keep the charts and other decorations on the walls to no more than two-thirds of the wall space. Choose rugs with simple or no patterns.

- Be thoughtful when it comes to smells. Be aware of smells/ odors that may trigger memories of tough experiences (e.g., aftershave, perfume, food smells). There is a strong connection to our memories through our olfactory senses. This can activate a child's nervous system if they smell things their brain associates with negative experiences. This is implicit memory; the child may not know a smell has activated their system. You might notice that a child becomes dysregulated about the same time there are food smells for lunch if your classroom is close to a cafeteria or if you are preparing a snack. That student may have had tough experiences around food. They were perhaps living without access to food or having food weaponized as punishment by a caregiver.

- Classroom lighting can be something to pay attention to for regulating nervous systems. Many classrooms use bright fluorescent lights. These can be overwhelming for some. Using effective but dimmable lights can help soothe some students. Yet, for others, dimming the lights may activate their nervous systems, especially if they have been sexually or physically abused in low light.

- Be mindful of the sounds introduced into the classroom and how they impact children. Sound can soothe or irritate any of us. Playing softer mood music before class begins or during nap time can help regulate moods. Loud sounds like fire drills or the chimes we use to get a student's attention can be enough to dysregulate a student for hours. Noise from air-conditioners, fans, and open windows can cause competition in our hearing ability.

It is important to connect the dots. For example, considering classroom sounds and noise, a child from a tough place may have difficulty separating all the auditory sensory information. They may want to listen to what is being said by their teacher or classmates but can't get past the competing sounds. These sounds may also add stimuli to an already overstimulated nervous system, which might be problematic. If we have a fire drill or lockdown drill and immediately find a student struggling with challenging behaviors, the noise and the student's struggle might be related. On the flip side, it may be that the student is accustomed to chaos and noise and is now placed in silence. This, too, can alert the nervous system if the environment is out of a child's norm. It can be important to recognize that nap time, quiz time, or quiet reading time may be uncomfortable for a child when their nervous system interprets that quiet as a threat. Quiet can activate the nervous system or signal threats for some students. If they come from a chaotic home, silence may be scary or feel like the calm before the storm for them. They may disrupt class because they cannot handle the quiet. If chaos is familiar, the brain likes it. They will seek to regulate through disruptive behaviors to return to something familiar. We must see communication in behavior. It is sometimes the only way a child has to tell us they are not okay.

Movement is regulating

The next issue to concentrate on for regulated classrooms is movement. Being asked to sit for hours is extremely abnormal for a child, yet it is a common demand for children in many Western cultures. When they can't sit still, they are punished for disrespect or insubordination or tested and medicated for ADHD or defiance disorders. Children are meant to move, run, dig their hands in the dirt, and be curious about the world around them. We have many double standards for children versus adults. Standing, for example, has a different expectation for adults, encouraged by employers who use standing desks and walking meetings. Yet we expect children to sit for hours, facing front and being quiet and obedient. It just isn't natural. Adults also have mental health days; children do not.

Not only do children and youth need movement "breaks," they also need movement added as part of the lessons. Movement allows for regulation of the brain's lower regions, allowing access to higher brain regions. Movement is vital to access the cortex, where higher learning and processing occur. Use patterned, rhythmic, repetitive strategies like Bal-A-Vis-X (see Appendix A), or other games and activities students can access to improve learning and creativity. This concept can be seen in action in everyday life. When do our best ideas come to us? When we're brushing our teeth? In the shower? Taking a walk? These activities involve patterned, rhythmic, and repetitive movement and help us access the ideas and learning part of the brain in the cortex.

Relate

We need to set up classrooms focused on belonging. By this point, we hope it is clear this is relational and often emotional work. For a child to access their learning brain, they need to be in settings where they feel that they belong. This is essential work where large portions of the population live in relational poverty. This is where using restorative approaches and practices becomes a lifeline for educators. Restorative work focuses on building a healthy relational climate in your classroom.

First, we need to define what we mean by relationship. All too often, we might believe that a relationship with a learner means knowing them well. But relationships need reciprocity to be healthy. Knowing our students well but our students not knowing us won't cut it. Instead, students need to be able to know us enough to be able to trust us. And we need to be able to trust them. This is done through an attuned and grounded adult utilizing unconditional, positive regard for students, regardless of their emotional state. Lori Desautels (2020), in her book *Connections Over Compliance: Rewiring Our Perceptions of Discipline*, states that:

> Relationships create healthy brain development and nervous systems that are calm and regulated. When an adult is emotionally

available, consistent, and present, this interpersonal intervention can damp down the stress response systems that have been accessing the higher cortical areas of the brain. This gives the student space to think, problem solve, emotionally regulate, pause, pay attention, and hold memories. (p.78)

Along with a healthy relationship with the adults in the classroom, students also need to have a healthy relationship with each other. Restorative practices aim to build, maintain, repair, and enhance relationships. Proactive practices like respect agreements (Brummer & Thorsborne 2020), community-building circles, and restorative chats can create connections with others and minimize the likelihood of ruptures. Creating a respect agreement in the classroom will also allow students to define what respect means for them, especially when we may be pushing for a version of respect incompatible with a student's cultural identity. Utilizing the circle process is one of the most effective ways of creating a classroom community built on respect. These practices also offer us strategies to model accountability and repair those relationships.

The circle process has been a part of the human journey for thousands of years. Early humans may have been drawn to circles around the fire because it was used for warmth and protection. The circle process developed as they gathered around the fire, passing on traditions, telling stories, and settling conflicts. Circles can be found in spiritual traditions around the globe, from the Māori people of New Zealand and Pacific Islands to the First Nation peoples of the Americas, Australia, and African nations. The circle seems to have always been a part of the human experience. Modern restorative circles are born from the traditions of *Indigenous* peoples. These traditions may vary depending on where we live and how these traditions have evolved.

For our purposes in the classroom, there are three major types of circles: community building, healing, and academic (see Brummer & Thorsborne 2020). Each follows similar stages and uses the same elements in their practice. In most circle traditions, there is a welcoming statement to begin the circle, followed by an opening tradition like reading a poem or playing a song. In Hawaiian traditions, all public gatherings begin with a traditional Hawaiian chant. These traditions are often patterned, rhythmic, and repetitive. They are regulating. The opening may involve movement like an icebreaker game or a mixer. There may then be a check-in round where students can relate to and empathize with the emotional states of others in the circle with them. A "get to know you" question is often asked to deepen those relationships. Values are identified and agreed on to bond the group further and create trust. Then, we are ready to dive into the content or reason for our circle. We follow regulate, relate, and reason (see Table 6.1).

Table 6.1: Stages of circle process

Welcome Mindful moment Opening tradition (song, chant, poem) Movement	Regulate
Check-in questions Get to know you rounds Icebreakers	Relate
Content or reason for circle • Community building • Healing or addressing harms • Academic circles	Reason/Reflection
Closing traditions	Regulate

Reason and reflection

This brings us to a trauma-informed approach to our curriculum and lesson planning. According to Dr. Bruce Perry, we need a curriculum that matches his six Rs that represent the key elements of positive developmental and educational settings (Graner & Perry 2023). It needs to be relevant, rewarding, rhythmic, repetitious, relational, and respectful. What does each of these mean in action?

Relevant

When we have relevant learning materials, each student can see how this material is useful and meaningful to their life. The material or lesson can overlap with other things the student cares about or is interested in. It also means that the materials match the child's emotional stage, which may differ from the chronological age. Trauma can interrupt and stunt development. A child may be ten years old chronologically but display the emotional age of a seven-year-old. Making the material match their functional age and tapping their interests will be more impactful. When information has relevance, it means it matters to the student. For example, math lessons will not feel relevant to a child who is hungry, tired, or unsafe. The promise of a sticker or reward to a child feeling pressured or forced to perform is also unlikely to be relevant.

Rewarding

Materials and lessons also need to be rewarding, and when we say rewarding, we mean implicit, internal rewards that are pleasurable, satisfying, and challenging enough, not stickers and prizes. We do this by getting to know children's interests and curiosity, and presenting material in ways that bring them interest and joy. This helps develop self-directed motivation.

Rhythmic

We also benefit by making lessons rhythmic because rhythm soothes and regulates the lower parts of our brains. When this happens, we have better access to higher brain regions—the cortex—where cognition and learning happen. Making lessons more rhythmic will help. Those who speak in rhythmic patterns are considered easier to listen to. Adding drumming, hand clapping, or walking while learning can increase interest and memory (see Appendix B, Drumming in the Torres Strait, for example). Music is the most powerful source of rhythm we can find as it is patterned, repetitive, rewarding, and, most importantly, rhythmic. Playing soft music in the classroom can help with learning; it regulates and creates a safe atmosphere.

Repetitious

Repetition is essential to creating and changing neural pathways. This is based on the idea that "cells that fire together wire together," which we first raised in Chapter 3 when we explored the need for repetition to change behavior. If you repeatedly *see* and *hear* a dog barking, with enough repetitions, you will no longer need to *see* the dog if you can hear it barking to *know* it's a dog barking! When neurons repeatedly fire together, they can be processed by the brain fully, even if not all the information is present. This creates a sense of predictability for children, fostering feelings of felt safety.

Respectful and relational

Our lessons also need to be respectful and relational. These two go hand-in-hand as we cannot have one without the other. Trauma-informed and restorative educators prioritize relationships. It takes an attentive, present, attuned, and responsive caregiver (educator) to meet the irreducible needs of a child (Perry 2020). By this point in the book, we hope you can see the relational nature of trauma-informed and restorative schools. Practices like circles, respect agreements, and restorative chats work to build relational classrooms. Respect needs to be our default in the classroom. We need to move away from this notion that students must earn it. We offer respect from the moment we first interact with another individual because it honors our unique humanity. This type of respect says, "I see you, hear you, and value your experience."

When we create a classroom in harmony with the sequential nature of the brain structure and function, we lower the chances of behavioral issues and increase the chance of learning through relationships. This is vital to calling ourselves trauma-informed restorative educators.

C.L.I.M.B. is an example of a regulated classroom and a restorative practice from Mayflower Mill Elementary in the state of Indiana in the United States (see Appendix D). Educators there have created an alternative classroom that replaces suspension and is incredibly restorative. Remember, being restorative is not a program but a way of being. This program is a good example of restorative practice in action.

CENTRAL IDEAS

★ Our brain is a prediction machine using interoception, sensory data, and experience to predict future needs it may have. If our past experiences are filled with trauma, we are more likely to predict something is a threat, even if that is perceived rather than actual.

★ Trauma is not what happens to us; it is the response of our nervous system to events. The three Es are an easy way to understand trauma: the event, the experience, and the effects.

★ Our current culture for children is toxic and, in many cases, traumatizing. We have essentially normalized things that traumatize children as something they "need," when in fact these things are harmful to their development.

★ Children's mental health has declined for many years, with increased anxiety, depression, and suicide. Children are feeling less safe at school.

★ Our brains are state-dependent, requiring us to account for that in the classroom. If we focus on regulation and relationships, we have an increased chance of learning.

★ Resilience is built through predictable, moderate, controllable stress that utilizes adult buffers to help our students build problem-solving skills. The dose (level of intensity) and space (how much time in between doses of stress) matter in building either sensitivity to stress or resilience. Our interventions must also be dosed and spaced to build healing and resilience.

★ Following the sequence of engagement (regulate, relate, reason) needs to be the structure of our classroom environment if learning is to occur.

  - Classrooms must provide a regulating environment for our students. In addition to how students are treated, they also need an environment with more safety cues than threat cues, and opportunities to move their bodies.

  - Our classrooms need to be relational, where students don't just fit in, they belong. Restorative practices are a homerun to make this happen.

  - Following the six Rs in the classroom will make our pedagogy more impactful.

REFLECTION QUESTIONS

✓ When we predict that a teacher will like us, and they do, it is reward-ing. The opposite might happen when we predict that our teacher will not like us; it is not rewarding. How do you create relationships with the students who think you do not like them?

✓ What parts of our school might not be healthy for a developing brain? What might you change in the school day to change those things?

✓ Describe the role of technology in your classroom. Is it creating safety cues or threats in the school day? What would you change?

✓ How aware are you of the little "t" traumas you have seen your students struggling with?

✓ What regulating strategies are you using in your classroom to help students maintain their state of regulation? What strategies keep you regulated as the adult in the room?

✓ Is your classroom sensitive to sensory needs? Consider colors, light-ing, smell, and clutter. Is there a regulation corner or room?

✓ What strategies will you use to bring more movement into your lessons? How often do you schedule brain breaks in your lessons?

✓ What creates a sense of belonging in your classroom? Do students see each other as supports or competitors?

✓ What is the role of restorative practices like circle or respect agree-ments in your classroom? How do you deepen students' connections to each other and you?

✓ Describe how the six Rs show up in your pedagogy.

In our next chapter, we will explore restorative practices and how they fit into this journey of being trauma-informed and restorative. We compare these ancient yet innovative ideas to what we now con-sider traditional discipline. We continue with additional strategies for supporting a classroom environment that is regulated, relational, and where learning can thrive.

CHAPTER 7

Restorative Approaches: Translating Theory and Principles into Practice

In Chapter 2, we introduced the notion of resolving discipline issues and conflict differently, viewing challenging behavior through a lens of relational accountability and trying to understand it through a trauma-informed lens. Chapter 8 considers a shame-sensitive lens through which to view behavior. In this chapter, we describe the basics of restorative practice, as it might be applied in the classroom rather than the larger application of a whole-school approach. But first, a reminder about the philosophy of this humanistic approach to problem-solving and the challenges this can present to old, embedded thinking and habits. If you have leapfrogged chapters, as many readers do (no blame here!), it might be useful to go back to Chapter 2 and check out some of the basic thinking about traditional policy and practice.

Retributive, authoritarian approaches ask questions like:

- What happened?

- What rule/law/expectation was broken?

- Who's to blame?

- What punishment is deserved?

Retributive, authoritarian approaches fit firmly in the operant conditioning and contingency mindset of behaviorism—accountability that acts as a deterrent to the student and others ("Do this and you'll get that!"), teaching the student a lesson about what not to do and encouraging compliance.

A restorative approach views the same incident or behavior through a different lens and asks different questions:

- What happened?
- What were the circumstances that led to what happened?
- Who has been hurt?
- What are their needs?

A restorative approach is the essence of relational accountability. It is an approach that focuses on the harm done in an incident. It focuses on problem-solving, engaging all voices affected to find a way forward. The process (and the plan developed) *is* the consequence. Table 7.1 compares the two paradigms in more detail.

Table 7.1: Comparison of retributive and restorative paradigms

Retributive approach/process	Restorative approach/process
Focus is on those responsible	Focus is on the harm done in an incident
Consequences are decided, set, and graded in severity by school officials	Consequences are decided with those affected and with those responsible
Those responsible are removed from their classroom/school community and *dealt with*	Those responsible are managed and supported within their classroom/school community as far as possible
Those responsible are told what is to happen to them and what needs to be said or done to others. These are unilateral decisions, made by adults in positions of authority	Those responsible are asked to fix things and are helped to make amends for their behavior. How to fix and make amends is a decision made in collaboration with those who are involved *in* the problem
Those harmed have little control over the process and outcomes	Those affected are asked what needs to happen to repair the harm and to ensure future safeguards
The conversation is about the past	The conversation is about the past, present, and future
The dialogue is one way, abstract, and managed by designated officials	The dialogue is relevant and concrete, and is facilitated by teachers and/or skilled students

Support groups and families are often viewed as part of the problem	Support groups and families are significant in rejecting behavior while supporting those responsible
Feelings and emotions are controlled and limited by school policy and protocol	Feelings and emotions are acknowledged and managed with dignity and respect
Shame is induced and used to disgrace those responsible	Shame is managed and discharged

Thorsborne and Vinegrad (2022, p.21). Reproduced with permission.

Here's another reminder about the basic philosophy of this *restorative justice* approach. In a nutshell, incidents of non-compliance/naughtiness/anti-social behavior in a school are viewed as a violation of people and relationships. This violation creates obligations and liabilities, and justice seeks to heal and make things right.

This inherently fair approach sees accountability in a different light. Not the orthodox/traditional notions of holding someone accountable by meting out a retributive consequence. Rather, it is a kind of accountability *process* that is way more genuine and confronting (more about this shortly).

David Karp and Marilyn Armour (2019) describe the underlying principles of this very different approach:

- *Inclusive decision-making:* Those who did "it" and those who had "it" done to them understand the problem better than someone outside the problem, and, therefore, it makes sense that they are invited to participate in the problem-solving.

- *Active accountability:* This is a face-to-face encounter that places the community of people *in* the problem *in the same room* so that the stories around what happened can be better understood (why and how it happened) and how people have been harmed—harm to individuals and harm to relationships—so this group can reach a shared understanding of stories, circumstances, and impacts.

- *Repairing the harm:* When it comes time for planning a way forward, healing of those harms is a priority, along with the support needed for anyone in the process, including the person who may have been responsible, making healing an inevitable expectation when ruptures to relationships occur.

- *Rebuilding trust:* Trust is the glue that holds healthy relationships together. Over time, trust is often eroded incrementally with relationship ruptures, and restoration will also take time.

Why does this restorative approach hold such a lure? For many reasons—some outlined in Table 7.1, and because punishment *has no capacity to heal.* We want our students to have the skills to manage themselves and their relationships as they enter the adult world and even when they are still at school because we seek the kind of genuine cooperation and collaboration that produces compliance as an outcome of a sense of community rather than an end in itself.

We strive to make a difference with the next generation, who will become employers, employees, parents, partners, neighbors, community members, politicians, and other key decision-makers. This means we must seriously rewire our brains, develop different habits, and realize how we have been socialized within and by our own cultures, families, nations, and religions. Take a moment to reflect on where you might land in the social discipline relationship window in Figure 7.1, developed first in a probation setting. It is an iconic framework explaining different mindsets about discipline. It helps us understand the challenges of holding each other accountable within a support framework.

Which quadrant best described how mistakes and conflict were handled by:

- your parents/caregivers? Did they share the same beliefs about child-rearing? If their beliefs were different, how did you navigate that as a child?

- your faith? What does it teach about accountability?

- the schools you attended?

Where would you place yourself now if you have been in education for some time? Which quadrant were you in when you started? What has happened that has changed your mind? What do you think now about power, support, and expectations? Compliance?

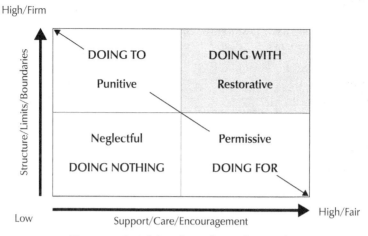

Figure 7.1: Social discipline relationship window
THORSBORNE AND VINEGRAD (2022, P.23). ADAPTED FROM WACHTEL (1999).

A LITTLE HISTORY

Historically, early restorative practice in schools (in the mid-90s) was limited to what we sometimes refer to as "pointy end" incidents of serious harm that usually resulted in suspensions/stand-downs/fixed-term exclusions or possibly criminal charges. This process is largely known as a *formal* restorative conference or formal repairing-harm circle, seen on the right end of the restorative continuum (see Figure 7.2). Brave practitioners have tackled any number of tricky issues that arise in schools: serious bullying, violence, threats of harm, serious destruction of property, abusive social media, a protracted conflict that often may have its origins in the community outside the school gates, harassment of all sorts, racial vilification, play that has got seriously out of hand and caused injury, extreme disrespectful behavior towards adults, theft. Does this list of incidents look familiar? Before you panic about whether or not the classroom teacher will be called on to facilitate any one of these at the serious end of the range of challenging incidents, our aim here is to help you understand what it is you *can* do in your classrooms to keep the small things small and, in a sense, minimize your need to refer small incidents on to administration. We call this DIY—Do It Yourself. Students hold more respect for educators who are conflict-competent.

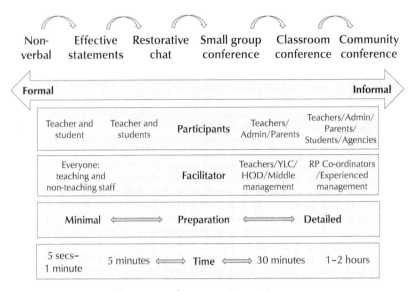

Figure 7.2: The restorative continuum
THORSBORNE AND VINEGRAD (2022, P.14).

Thorsborne and Vinegrad (2022) note in their book *The Continuum of Restorative Practices in Schools: An Instructional Training Manual for Practitioners* a change in terminology from "Affective Statements to Effective Statements" and that effective statements:

> ...integrate and engage a wider range of practices that are known and recognized as behavior management strategies. Effective statements include non-verbal and verbal prompts, hints, gestures, cues, reminders, redirections, affective statements etc. How these statements are delivered is just as important as their content and in a relational classroom the focus will be on using the least intrusive strategy, delivered respectfully, so that we can keep the small stuff small. (p.14)

As described elsewhere (Thorsborne, in press), practitioners worldwide have adapted their processes for elementary and very young students (kindergarten and preschool), those with diverse needs, small group "mini-conferences" and large group classroom conferences/circles for the daily grind issues that emerge in classrooms. Many of the processes also developed would be described as preventative—laying the foundations of expectations and agreements about how we would want our classrooms to look, sound, and feel (Brummer & Thorsborne 2020; Finnis 2021; Smith, Fisher, & Frey 2022; Thorsborne & Vinegrad 2022) along with more relational approaches to pedagogy that focus on genuine engagement and mutual trust and respect.

This approach, however, does assume some skills and mindsets for educators. Do we:

- work to *really* know our students? (Enough to know their challenges and their family's challenges? What are their likes and dislikes, struggles, achievements, and goals?)

- make time to develop social capital (Aliaksei 2020)[1] with and between our students to develop a safe space for them (and us) so trust is built?

- respect all our students in ways that matter to them (that is, value them for who they are and understand that many disrespectful behaviors we see might result from our (unintentional) or implicit lack of respect for them?

- model the behaviors we expect our students to learn?

- teach them, with patience and repetition, the skills they might not yet have acquired?

- realize that changing the behavior of our students means our approach must change first and that we must move on from theories built on behaviorism to more humanistic approaches?

- use acknowledgment (we have 'noticed') and encouragement rather than rewards, working on developing intrinsic motivation?

- realize there is no such thing as a quick fix and there are no shortcuts to rewiring our or others' neural pathways/habits?

- understand that behavior is what we can *see* on the outside, the symptom of what might be happening *in* the brain; that it might be evidence of a lack of skill or what might have helped them survive in the past?

---

1   Social capital is variously described as social relationships, networks, and structures that build a sense of trust and reciprocity.

- make ourselves available to work things out with and between students without relying on punitive consequences?

- take the time to solve problems, even though it might look as if we don't have enough time?

- know ourselves well enough and are we reflective enough to know our triggers and biases?

- Do we know when we need some professional support?

- respond calmly?

- do less talking and more listening?

- take care of our wellness (see Chapter 5) so that we are in a good, steady place to manage our relationships with colleagues and students?

THE RESTORATIVE SEQUENCE

The following section describes what we know as essential components or sequences/steps that apply generally to any restorative process, as illustrated in Figure 7.3. The details here are described in brief.

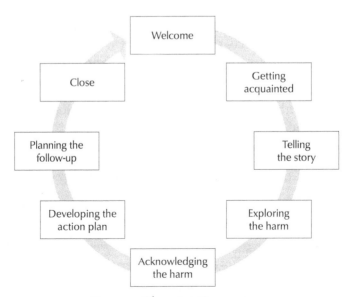

Figure 7.3: The restorative sequence

Greater detail is provided elsewhere in the myriad of training manuals and texts written about restorative practices in schools (Brummer & Thorsborne 2020; Thorsborne & Vinegrad 2022; Finnis 2021) and published in many education department/ministry websites worldwide. To be effective, this sequence in the facilitated dialogue must be preceded by careful investigation of the facts and preparation of the individuals in the process. This serves the purpose of managing expectations about the process (its form and purpose) and the rules of engagement. It prepares us, if we are facilitating, for anything raised in the meeting. Follow-up is also important to ensure that the plan is working, or if it isn't, addressing any barriers that have surfaced. Again, the details of preparation and follow-up are explored in the resources we have mentioned.

However, nothing of any use can be achieved unless the student and you, the educator, are regulated—that is, calm. This also includes the parent(s) if they are participating in a problem-solving dialogue. Understanding Dr. Bruce Perry's fundamental advice about regulating, relating, and—only then—reasoning is a critical component for successful problem-solving. The restorative sequence emphasizes the need to be curious, not furious, to be prepared to explore rather than explode, and always seek to understand before being understood.

The invitation

In a general sense, the restorative approach involves a sequence that usually begins with an invitation to see the process as *an opportunity to make sense of what happened* rather than to lay blame or sit in judgment about the people in the problem, whether or not they might be good or bad, or to tell them off. It attempts to understand what harm has happened, and how that harm might be addressed. There is agency/autonomy in this approach—students and adults participate voluntarily (some, to be sure, reluctantly at first), and we need to be genuinely invitational in our approach. Michelle Stowe's list of "restorative sound bites" (2023), mentioned in Chapter 2, focuses on invitational ways to engage with a young person when problem-solving is needed. Here's another example of a relational invitation with one or a couple of students: "I am hoping to ask you some questions; you can ask me them too. Are you open to that?"

It's worthwhile checking out other "bites" on her blog to get a general idea about how to frame the invitation to participate in problem-solving. These invitations serve two purposes: first, they help in the regulation process because they show genuine interest, and second, they demonstrate "connect before correct." Ross Greene's collaborative and proactive approach to problem-solving empathy step is also deeply invitational by saying something like "I notice that you're having difficulty moving from recess back into the classroom. What's up?" (Green 2021, p.70). Both demonstrate a deep interest, as opposed to being judgmental. Judgment and a telling-off will likely stifle genuine dialogue as the student's brain moves to fight, fight, or freeze.

Welcome and introductions

At the start of the meeting, the facilitator will welcome participants into the process, perform introductions where needed, and proceed to remind everyone about the purpose of the meeting and the rules of engagement. This will help to begin settling the anxiety that is likely to be in the room.

Telling the story about what happened

The next step of the exploratory sequence explores "what happened?" and usually starts with the person responsible. Every person *in a problem* (those who did it and those who had it done to them) has a different perspective, so discovering our narratives is vital to reaching a shared understanding of the big picture. There are stories within stories, and the only way to make sense of what happened is to create the space for these stories to be told. Simple questions might include:

- What happened? How did this unfold? What happened next?

- How did you get involved?

- Where did it start to go wrong for you?

Understanding the motivation/intention

This part of the sequence is to uncover or get to the bottom of how the incident happened *without* asking, "Why did you do that?" The *why* question is often experienced as judgmental and accusatory, so it is best to use different versions to discover "why." It is also likely that with young people not used to deeper reflections about their behavior, all you get is a shrug or "I dunno." It is very much a part of making sense of what happened for *everyone* listening. It also signals any underlying problems and lack of skill, which is vital for long-term problem-solving. It is not for us to judge the wrongness or rightness of what happened but to remain curious. What usually works best are questions like:

- What were you thinking when...?

- What was going on for you when...?

- What was the purpose of that?

- What were you hoping would happen?

- What did you want to happen? (Especially useful for young students.)

(Please note here that if the challenging behaviors originated in trauma responses such as the autonomic nervous system's fight, flight, or freeze, the young person might not know their "why" or have any explicit memory of the event. We cannot assume they are lying.)

The next part of the process asks those responsible to consider who might have been affected and how to use questions like:

- Who has been affected by what happened?

- How have they been affected?

- What do you think it is like for...when that happens?

- Who else might have been affected?

These questions are invitations to look outward beyond self, not inward, and to link behaviors to the consequences for others, realizing the impacts on others when we have done something that has caused a rupture.

Exploring the harm

It is now the turn of those affected to tell their story—not just to the person responsible but to *everyone else* attending the process. The questions asked of them (both those directly affected and their supporters if present) look similar:

- What happened from your perspective?

- What did you think when it happened/was happening?

- When you thought about it later, what did you make of it?

- How has this been for you?

- What has been the worst/most difficult/hardest?

You should have noted by now that these questions are mostly open-ended, exploratory, and curious. *How* they are asked will also make a difference. There is no room for sarcasm, loaded questions, lectures, or too many closed questions. These questions must be asked calmly and respectfully with genuine interest, no matter how exasperated we feel. Remember the power of contagion and, at that moment, the need to be regulated.

When the people in the problem can reach a shared understanding and make sense of the reasons/intention/motivation for the behavior and the collective harm caused, this process will likely generate understanding and empathy as they hear these stories. This is not a one-way process but happens for everyone present, helping them to connect through shared perspectives and, often, shared pain.

One of the more interesting parts of the process, when done well, is the dawning awareness that several people/issues may have contributed to what went wrong (e.g., a student may have been late to class, and their teacher had publicly called them out in front of others; the student response was disrespectful). In unpacking what happened, the teacher can hear for the first time what had happened that made the student late. The teacher can also hear what had been happening to them and how stressed/dysregulated they were. The student gets to hear how the teacher's response to the lateness contributed to what happened next. We call this *collective responsibility*, which leads to *collective accountability*.

Acknowledgment

These are useful questions at this point to ask the person/people responsible:

- Now that you have heard from...what do you think about what you did (or how you contributed to the problem) and how you affected others?

- Now that you have heard from everyone, what do you realize now?

We hope for something like "I didn't realize," "I didn't intend to hurt you/scare you," or "I feel bad about what I did." These are expressions of remorse, guilt, and empathy. This may or may not include an apology. We take for granted that young people know the purpose of an apology and how and when to make one. The apology skill is a complex social skill (very much influenced by culture) and needs to be taught. Many adults have not acquired this skill or awareness of possible cultural differences. It is also important for the adult to acknowledge what *they* hadn't realized or how their actions also had consequences. Harm is rarely unidirectional in the petri dish of a classroom.

Genuine, empathic acknowledgment allows those harmed some relief ("Finally, I am understood.") and those responsible a sense of not being judged as a bad person. If this sense of relief is reached, then the process is poised to begin developing a plan focused on making things right and beginning the problem-solving process around the contributing factors. The brainstem, diencephalon, and limbic brain have been navigated successfully, and everyone's cortex (the brain's rational part) is open to problem-solving.

Planning for what's next

The process so far has dealt with the past and the present. Now, it is time to consider the future. In the restorative space, the most urgent part of the plan is about what's needed to make things right for those harmed. In other words, how do we repair the damage that's been done? Helpful questions might include:

- How can this be made right? What do you need to feel... (respected/safe)?

- What do you need to feel supported?

- What suggestions do you have that will help?

- What are you prepared to commit to?

This is very much a negotiation among those present. First, to make things right; second, to put things in place to minimize the chance of "it" happening again (getting at the root causes, including system failures); and third (and equally important), to follow up. These plans need to be specific, practical, and explicit, ideally recorded somewhere to indicate how seriously the issue has been taken. It is important that the adult is not *telling* the student/s what is in the plan but *asking* what might work. Giving young people some autonomy/agency is likely to increase commitment to the plan.

While this process, at least in print, looks easy to follow, all the pieces that make the whole are nuanced. Reading from a list of questions does not make the process relational if it is mechanical, not genuine, or not backed up with a relational mindset. Training and practice will help you to become competent and confident in managing the subtleties. Where possible, spend time with others with more experience and be prepared to seek support and feedback.

The 5 skills of restorative

In our previous book, *Building a Trauma-Informed Restorative School: Skills and Approaches for Improving Culture and Behavior* (Brummer & Thorsborne 2020), we dedicated a chapter to each of the Five Skills of Restorative: mindfulness, empathy, honest expression, questions, and the art of requests. This section provides an overview of these skills and encourages you to dive deeper as your journey into this work continues. The Five Skills of Restorative (see Figure 7.4) outlines the more discrete skills embedded in what we increasingly understand is the gamut of restorative practices. Every strategy is clearly explained and adapted to be appropriate for children and adults who have experienced trauma.

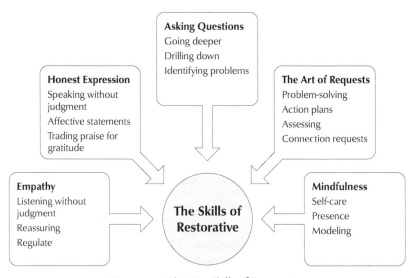

Figure 7.4: The Five Skills of Restorative
BRUMMER AND THORSBORNE (2020, P.84).

Mindfulness

We will start with *mindfulness*, as none of the other skills are helpful unless we can use those skills with presence and intention. Mindfulness is both a skill and a practice. We need to be able to show up and be present for ourselves. It is the skill that is foundational to all the other restorative skills. To offer empathy and deeply listen, we need to be present, attentive, and connected to another human if we are to hear them truly.

Mindfulness is crucial for adults to be capable of co-regulating a child. We need to be in touch with our nervous system state because we will share that with those around us. If we are dysregulated, we will dysregulate others, including children. That also means if we are calm and regulated, we have that state to share with a child needing co-regulation. This constant skill of checking in with our state requires daily practice. It requires us to practice being aware of ourselves, our breath, our bodies, and our state. It requires acknowledging our sensations of hunger, thirst, alertness, sleepiness, and even our emotional states, without judgment. Learning to be gentle with ourselves is to be mindful of our hearts.

There are two major approaches to mindfulness. Our first is a formal practice of sitting in meditation. This is a regular focused attention practice where we allow our attention to stay present to a single focused thing. It could be a mantra we repeat over and over in our minds. It could be focusing our attention on our breath or our heartbeat. It could be humming and allowing our mind to focus on the humming or sounds around us. Our second approach is daily informal practice. This is the practice of doing things with our full attention on what we are doing. When we brush our teeth, we focus our energy on each tooth as we brush. If we are eating mindfully, it means savoring and staying present in each bite, maybe focusing on where that food came from. How did it grow? Who picked it? Who drove it to the store where might we purchase it? We take in the fullness of the task using curiosity and focused attention.

The events often hijack the attention of many people who have experienced adversity and trauma. Rather than being able to focus attention on the task at hand, the brain has been wired by experience to stay hypervigilant to dangers. That divides our attention. Practicing mindfulness can give educators and students who have experienced traumatic situations a chance to learn to shift and control their attention.

Focused attention practices can also become a part of our school day to get a stronger focus on preventing behavior issues. These practices, done by students and educators, can regulate our nervous systems, allowing us to better support student learning. Add focused attention practices at set times like the beginning of the school day, during the morning circle, before or after lunch, before a quiz or exam, or near the end of the school day. Regularly finding time to support nervous system regulation through breathing or moving will greatly reduce behavior issues.

Empathy

Our next skill is *empathy*, which is heavily influenced by Marshall Rosenberg's work in Nonviolent Communication. In our first book (Brummer & Thorsborne 2020), we wrote:

> Restorative requires deep listening. This is a form of listening that requires our whole person. To listen mindfully requires us to give the

speaker our full presence, taking in body language, facial expressions, and tone of voice. It requires us to hear beyond the spoken words so we can hear the basic universal needs that those words decode for us. (p.95)

Most of us have been exposed to various forms of listening techniques like reflective listening, active listening, or empathic listening. In the world of restorative, we need all those techniques because some work better depending on the situation or setting.

Our current educational environments, if built on punitive discipline, discourage children from being honest with us. They tend to live with the underlying fear of "getting in trouble" instead of being seen as "in-struggle." We may need to reassure them they are not in trouble and that our goal is to support them with the problem or behaviors that need to change. It is hard to solve problems when you cannot converse honestly about those behaviors. A lack of executive function or just lagging skills can leave children with unsolved problems and behaviors they are stumped on how to solve. Training ourselves to hear the human needs left unmet by those problems can be life-saving support for children who struggle with behavior issues. Behind the big feelings and emotions that can lead to outbursts are unmet needs waiting to be addressed. Empathy is about finding and connecting with those needs. We can't always meet them, yet we can shine a light on them so a child feels seen, heard, and valued.

To truly listen deeply, we must be thoughtful about our intentions to be sure our goal is connection rather than fixing, debating, or competing with our speaker. Even more important is our ability to stay mindful of our nervous systems when we become activated and perhaps defensive. If our goal is to solve their problem, we are likely more in our heads looking for solutions rather than listening. If our goal is to debate them, we may find ourselves thinking of how to prove them wrong. If we are out to compete, we will look for ways to be one-up on their experience with one of our own. These attempts to control our speaker usually come with good intentions yet still fail at true connection.

Lots of roadblocks come to us when trying to listen as humans. The first is dysregulation. We don't listen well when we are dysregulated, primarily because we lose our ability to take another's perspective when we lose access to our cortex. Other roadblocks to listening would be falling into fix-it or defensive mode (rooted in fight or flight and shame). When we are in fix-it mode, we have been trapped by our discomfort of someone else's pain. We try to fix or solve the other person's pain to relieve our suffering (see Table 7.2). It is easy to fall into this because we tend to see young humans as helpless, and it is often faster and easier for us to solve it for them. This keeps us in the "Doing for" box of the social discipline relationship window (see Figure 7.1). We use a variety of tactics we may believe it the moment are helpful but, in reality, are not.

Table 7.2: Examples of fix-it solutions

Approach	Sounds like this...
Advising	"I think you should..." "Why don't you..."
One-upping or "stacking the deck"	"That's nothing; wait till you hear what happened to me!" or "You think you've got it bad."
Educating	"This could turn into a very positive experience for you if you just..." or "What did you learn from that?" or "That's not a feeling."
Consoling	"It wasn't your fault; you did the best you could" or "Why would anyone do that to you?"
Commiserate	"Oh, I don't like her either" or "I feel the same way about math."
Lecturing	"I have told you a million times that this sort of behavior..."
Storytelling	"When I was your age..." or "I know what you mean; it's just like when..."
Shutting down	"Cheer up. Don't feel so bad" or "Don't get mad..."
Sympathizing	"Oh, you poor thing..." or "I feel so sorry for you."
Interrogating	"When did this happen?" or "Who was it?"
Explaining	"I would have called but..." or "Let me explain why this happens."
Correcting	"That's *not* how it happened" or "You mean *last* week?"

Adapted and modified from Rosenberg (2015, pp.92–93).

The next trap past fix-it happens when our nervous systems are activated into fight or flight, often without our awareness. In this trap, we can become defensive or competitive. This is based on our dysregulation from perceiving the other person's issues as different from our personal view. In this mode, we may fail to remember that the other person's experience is unique to them, possibly very different from our own. Remember that our perceptions of the world around us are filtered through every experience we have ever had; that is, we each experience the present moment through the lens of interoception, sensory data, and our past. It can look like Table 7.3.

Table 7.3: Examples of competition/defensiveness statements

Approach	Sounds like this...
Competition/ defensiveness	"You're WRONG! and I am RIGHT and, even if I am not right, I am going to prove you are wrong anyway" or "You know that's not how it happened" or "Oh, Mrs. Smith doesn't hate you."
Revenge	"You don't know what you are talking about" or "Does anyone have any intelligent questions?" or "I'll teach you to talk back to me" or "How dare you speak to me like that!"
Silence to remain safe	"I am not talking to her until she apologizes."

Brummer and Thorsborne (2020, p.98).

When we listen using empathy as a skill, we need to be fully present for the other person, so we combine this skill with our mindfulness skill and practice. It may require us to remove distractions and regulate our systems by checking in with ourselves to be sure we can listen deeply. We follow a four-step approach developed by Marshall Rosenberg (2015): observation, feelings, needs, and requests (see Table 7.4). What is the speaker observing with no judgments, comparisons, or evaluations mixed in? What is the speaker feeling in the moment, and what met or unmet needs are those feelings coming from? What is the speaker requesting from us?

Table 7.4: Empathic listening

Approach	Sounds like this...
What other people are observing?	"Are you reacting to what Sally said about your paper?"

cont.

Approach	Sounds like this...
What are other people feeling and needing?	"Are you feeling disappointed because you would have liked more support preparing for the exam?"
"What are people requesting?"	"Are you asking for an explanation of why that was said?"

Brummer and Thorsborne (2020, p.99).

Honest expression

Often in the world of restorative, *honest expression* is referred to as "affective statements," which easily turn into blame and shame. Statements like these can sound like "When I saw you do X, I felt X..." and they send the message to students: "My feelings are your fault." As stated earlier in this chapter, we have renamed this *effective statements*, which again are influenced by the work of Marshall Rosenberg's practice of Nonviolent Communication, and utilize the skill of honest expression. Rosenberg managed to take the average "I" statement from an "I feel because you..." to "I feel because of my needs..." This removes blame and shame from our expression of our internal experiences. This is a way of connecting others to what is truly important to us: our universal human needs. These statements can be used to express when our needs are unmet, and express gratitude when our needs are met. This is a wonderful alternative to praising children. Praise for children who have been abused can be a cue for a threat, as praise may have been used as a grooming tool by an abuser. It is best to find alternatives to using praise if your goals are to be trauma-informed and restorative. These statements are easy and still require practice. They follow a simple yet powerful framework, demonstrated in Table 7.5.

Table 7.5: Effective statements

Element	Description	Example
Observation	We state our observations free of judgement, comparison, evaluation, or blame. We state what our senses see, hear, or smell.	"This is the third time this week I have seen you arrive ten minutes past our agreed start time."

Feelings	We name the feelings/ emotions we experience in response to our observation followed by the need or value that is either met or not met.	"I am feeling frustrated and disappointed because I have a need for punctuality and respect."
Needs		
Requests	We make a clear, specific, and timely request as to how that need could be met, completely willing to hear a "no" as there are many strategies to meet a need.	"Would you be willing to arrive at 9 a.m. for tomorrow's appointment?"

Questioning

Another skill in restorative is *questioning*, which is integral to getting children to talk to us, tell their stories, and supporting them in solving problems. It is not helpful when we use questions in problem-solving, such as accusing, interrogating, or judging. It is helpful when we borrow some techniques from mediators, so we ask questions that support drilling down on the problem instead of grilling the student as if they have done something "wrong." Questions should create connection, drill down on problems, identify and validate emotions, and seek clarity about words, amounts, or meaning.

In restorative work, we use questions to:

- *create connection:* our goal of communicating with a student must always focus on creating a connection

- *drill down to the problem:* we don't solve behaviors. We can use questions asked out of curiosity and connection to solve the issues that led to the behavior

- *identify emotions:* using *empathy guesses*, we can help students build a vocabulary of emotions while simultaneously teaching them social-emotional skills

- *seek clarity:* we also use questions to get clarity. Sometimes, this is about the meaning of particular words or just going deeper into the issue.

When asking questions, we must be mindful of *our* non-verbals, including body language, tone of voice, and even facial expressions.

The meaning and intention of a question can vary greatly simply by changing any of our non-verbals. It is also important we allow students processing time after asking a question. Little brains are not as fast as adult brains. They may need a few minutes to process the question or decide how to answer. Allow them time for that. Remember not to layer your questions on the student or ask multiple things at once. We do not want to overwhelm them.

Ask one question at a time and allow the student the opportunity to answer it before asking the next one. Layered questions require lots of working memory, and some children may struggle with that if they have been impacted by trauma. It is also suggested to have a path and direction for your line of questions so they feel relevant and open. We can ask questions about when their problems occur. We can ask questions that allow students to compare and contrast their problems in different situations. We can ask questions about the elements of a task to find where the problem might be. In our first book, we went into great detail about how to use these various types of questions.

Most importantly, our intention in using questions is more about creating a connection to the child's experiences and emotions than collecting data or answers. It is about their experience of the problem, not just finding a fix.

Here are some helpful types of questions to use in problem-solving with children:

- *Breakdown questions:* These questions take a large problem and break it down into smaller parts. We then list the smaller parts as a menu of possible smaller problems. For example, we might ask a child struggling with a science project what the hard part of the problem is. Is it picking the project? Getting the materials together? Is it gluing the pieces together?

- *Clarification questions:* These might ask our speaker to clarify what they may have meant by a particular word, phrase, or even amounts of percentages. For example, "I heard you say your mom was nurturing. What does nurturing look like for you? Was it lots of hugs? Food? Care?" Or maybe it is about checking in on time. For example, "I heard you say this is taking 'so much of your time.' How many hours would that be per week?"

- **Compare and contrast:** These questions ask about contradictions, opposites, variations, or exceptions. For example, "Why does the problem occur sometimes and not at other times?" or "When is the problem present and when is it not present?" or "What happens when we add or take away elements?"

- **Empathy guess:** This is as simple as asking the question, "Are you feeling 'X' because you need 'Y'?" or when someone is clearly upset, ask, "Are you feeling upset because you need more support?"

- **Observation of discrepancy:** These questions come from Ross Greene's book *Lost at School: Why Our Kids with Behavioral Challenges are Falling Through the Cracks and How We Can Help Them* (2014, p.83). These questions allow us to explore contradictions or even what may appear like dishonesty on the surface. We might ask a child, "Hey, I noticed you said you and Sean were getting along great, yet I heard you arguing yesterday at lunch. What's up with that?"

- **Relationship questions:** How are things related to each other? Ask, "I heard you mention Pokémon while talking about your homework. How does Pokémon play out when trying to do your homework?"

- **Scale questions:** Asking about the intensity of things on a scale of 1–5 or 1–10 can help us gauge a child's experience of a problem. For example, "On a scale of 1–5, with one being awful and five being awesome, how is your day?"

- **Verifying hunches:** As humans, we tend to make many assumptions about the world, which is our prediction system working to keep us safe. When we "assume" something, our brain tries to make sense of what is happening to determine if it is safe. Assumptions are not a problem unless we act on them. Try turning your assumptions into hunches you follow for clarification. See if what you assume is accurate or not. Ask about it!

- *Who, what, where, when, and how:* These basic questions seek basic content-related information. They are always helpful and are better than "why" questions.

We have two ways of framing a question, either open-ended or closed-ended. We need both of these and for different reasons. Open questions help us get more information when that is what we need. Closed questions help us get agreements. We must ask open-ended questions early in the problem-solving process, inviting speakers to give us more information, elaborate, or go deeper. "Tell me more about X?" or "Can you explain your experience with X?" or any question that doesn't ask for a specific answer. Closed questions ask for specific answers like a yes or a no. These are helpful when we want definite answers or clarity about what someone is unwilling to do. Closed questions help us form action plans and agreements.

Art of requests

Our last skill might be one of the hardest: the *art of requests*. This skill allows us to help children clean up their messes and take accountability for their actions in a compassionate and supportive manner that is non-punitive. It is also vital to the work that our action plans for children are trauma-informed, culturally informed, developmentally appropriate, and truly restorative rather than punitive.

The *art of requests* starts by understanding what it means to be accountable, as our request for repairing the harm is based on accountability for the harm created rather than an intervention that seeks to solve all the young person's issues. Requests must be strength-based and voluntary, or they are just punishments. They must allow students to make amends and restitution to themselves and others. We often skip this step for young people, teaching them self-forgiveness.

Next, those who harmed need to make things right with those directly harmed. This must be done in partnership with those directly harmed. Then, we need responsible youth to repay their community for bringing harm to those indirectly harmed, when appropriate. All of these agreements that create our action plan must be done collaboratively to balance the needs of those directly impacted, those indirectly impacted, and the responsible youth. Everyone impacted by an incident must have a seat in the circle with a voice that shares their needs.

All of these skills are life skills. They help us live a trauma-informed, restorative life. They help us connect with other humans in ways that foster relational rewards in our brains. They make our interactions with others less frustrating because they allow us to be more empathic and compassionate.

PULLING IT ALL TOGETHER

In a classroom, this *relational* approach becomes evident in the way we:

- greet, connect with, and welcome our students at the beginning of the day or to each lesson so they feel *seen*

- help individuals (or the whole class) become regulated before launching into the lesson

- develop consistent, repetitive routines that help promote predictability and regulation

- negotiate our mutual expectations of each other at the beginning of the term and with regular reminders—at the beginning of each lesson, if needed

- are prepared to invest in circle processes to develop social capital with and between learners

- adapt our approaches to pedagogy, including using circles to teach areas of the curriculum where appropriate

- know when to abandon the lesson and "circle-up" to address issues and behaviors affecting relationships and learning

- are prepared to acknowledge and apologize (where appropriate) for our own mistakes and miscalculations, which may have let our students down

- take the time to problem-solve with a student or a couple of students around their behaviors and issues. Depending on lesson activities and time, this may be during the lesson or later

- strive hard to "keep the small things small" and take responsibility, as far as we are skilled, to solve our in-class problems.

This list ties in with the advice we provided in Chapter 6 to assist in regulating a whole class to enhance the teaching and learning opportunities within a lesson.

We want to take the opportunity to be clear about what restorative practice *is* and *is not*.

- It *is not* a tool in our toolbox, nor a behavior management strategy.

- It *was not* designed to reduce re-offending. Our ancestors recognized the need to repair harm after an incident to protect the community, whether the quality of relationships in that community meant survival or not. Evaluation of quality processes in youth justice and school settings does point to *lessening the likelihood* of repeat and less serious behaviors.

- It *is not* used indiscriminately for some students, staff, and families and not others.

- It *is* a mindset about the "way we treat each other here."

- It *is* a relational *approach*, not a strategy.

- It *is* about strengthening relationships in the wake of an incident that has caused rupture and distance between those in the problem.

- It *requires* us, as adults, to be self-regulated so that we are curious, not furious, when in dialogue with others.

- It *is not* about lowering our standards around learning and behavior.

- It *is not* "offender" or "victim" centered. It engages the community of people affected in problem-solving along with those responsible. Think "incident" centered.

- It *requires* us, as adults, to take responsibility for our behavior that may have contributed to the problem; it *is not* about young people being the ones who are always wrong, and the adult is always right.

- It *is not* a quick fix. There is a recognition that behavior change is rarely instant; it takes repetition to rewire neural pathways and create new habits.

- As a process, it seeks to identify underlying issues that have contributed to the problem; it *is* tough on the problem but *not* on the people in it.

- It *is not* solely used to respond to wrongdoing; this relational approach has signaled the need to do the preventative work of connecting us, to build social capital, to build trust—these strategies will reduce the likelihood of us harming each other as they build a sense of community and belonging. We need to know there is something to restore to!

At this point, we hope you are reassured again that your beliefs about the need for positive, healthy relationships with learners are so right!

HOW RESTORATIVE AM I?

You might like to consider Table 7.6, at the end of this chapter. It is helpful to complete with someone you know and trust so there is a possibility of a fearless and frank conversation about your restorative development. Try the following questions with your partner after completing the table:

- What have you realized about your pattern of responses?

- Where do your strengths lie?

- What needs attention?

- How could you be supported to develop these skills?

Table 7.6: How relational am I? Thinking about my practice

Read the statements below to indicate how you resolve a challenging moment with a student. This exercise can be done in pairs with someone you trust. Use the scale: 1 (Rarely), 2 (Sometimes), 3 (Most of the time), 4 (Always) to respond to each statement.

Resolving a challenging incident: Talking it through...	1	2	3	4
1. I remain calm/regulated during the dialogue. I am curious, not furious.				
2. I know what's going on in this student's life.				
3. We talk in a private space.				
4. The student is calm and feeling safe (as far as I can tell). I wait until we are both regulated.				
5. I have made time for this.				
6. I have listened intently without interrupting.				
7. We both end up understanding the motivation/intention/triggers behind what happened. Our perspectives have changed.				
8. We have come to understand the damage (relational, emotional, physical); who has been harmed, and how.				
9. The student understands why he/she is "in trouble"; what rule has been broken; what the purpose of the rule is; what school/class values or expectations have been breached.				
10. I talked about how the problem is for me (where appropriate), after the student has had their turn.				
11. I take responsibility for any part I might have played in what went wrong and acknowledge that. I apologize for this.				
12. I accept an apology with grace.				
13. Together, we negotiated a plan. I have agreed to help if needed.				
14. The relationship with the student (or with the students and others) is repaired; I will check in to make sure.				
15. I have asked for someone I trust to observe my relational practice and give me honest feedback.				
16. I try to handle most issues/incidents myself, and only ask for help when I do not have the skills.				
17. Looking back on how I handled the situation, I could have benefited from some support.				

CENTRAL IDEAS

★ Restorative approaches focus on relational accountability and the healing of harm rather than punishment that is not empowered to heal or meet the needs of those harmed.

★ Restorative practice requires a rethink about how we have been socialized to view and respond to wrongdoing.

★ Restorative practice in education has evolved from restorative criminal justice approaches and has been adapted for a range of settings in schools.

★ Restorative processes focus on understanding the motivation underlying an incident, the harm caused to people and relationships, and making plans to heal these harms. The people *in* the problem are the ones who understand the problem the best, so their contributions to the process are vital. It is a community approach to problem-solving.

★ Successful restorative practice at the individual level is underpinned by specific skills and a mindset that include an understanding of the neuroscience of brains and behavior change.

REFLECTION QUESTIONS

✓ To what extent has the restorative approach challenged your ideas about responding to wrongdoing and accountability?

✓ How has your thinking about behavior change and problem-solving changed over time? What influenced this?

✓ Do you better understand the need to incorporate trauma-informed thinking into your practice? What do you need to do to achieve this?

✓ Can you explain to students and colleagues that the restorative approach is a *way of being* with others, a relational approach to prevention and intervention?

In our next chapter, we explore the impact of shame resulting from trauma, ruptured relationships when we blunder, and, more generally, when our expectations are not met. This will add another layer of understanding about our own and others' behavior and why restorative approaches suit how our brains work.

CHAPTER 8

Shame, Trauma, and Restorative Practice

Any discussion about trauma and self-regulation challenges would be incomplete without a brief discussion of the pervasiveness of *shame* and its impact on our behavior (adult or child). Shame is as ubiquitous as the air we breathe and such a common experience that we do not pay it nearly enough attention. Various experts who write about the impacts of chronic trauma refer to shame (Brown 2021; Conti 2021; Cozolino 2014; Maté & Maté 2022). In fact, Paul Conti, psychiatrist and author of *Trauma: The Invisible Epidemic*, mentions shame as an "accomplice" to trauma (2021, p.29). Focusing on shame here will help us better understand some behaviors we see in ourselves and others. And when we do notice, because it might have become intense, unless we know how to name it, we cannot make much sense of the feeling except to note how uncomfortable it is and how to limit its power over how we feel about ourselves.

Luna Dolezal and Matthew Gibson (2022), researchers from Exeter University and Birmingham University in the UK, respectively, argue that shame is a universal experience and that there is an increasing understanding of the impact of trauma and its capacity to trigger shame. In the same article, they urge those whose work involves trauma-informed approaches to develop *shame-sensitivity*. In a lengthy discussion about the acknowledgment of shame beyond a theoretical perspective, they argue for several issues to be addressed:

- The need for shame *competence:* developing an understanding of shame and its pervasiveness for anyone working in this space.

- Organizational understanding of shame: recognizing that some policies and procedures can shame staff and those on the other end of such policies and practices. Think about how shame-inducing some strategies are when dealing with discipline issues.

- Shame is behind much of the maladaptive and shame-defense behaviors associated with trauma: understanding that individual histories, culture, and community expectations will determine our experiences with shame and shaming.

In this chapter, we explore some neurobiology to explain how shame, dominant in our lives but not nearly understood well enough, can impact our exposure to high-stress or chronic events and situations. How we deal with it over time can become wired into our brains, or as Brené Brown describes in her interview with Oprah Winfrey in her *Super Soul Sunday* TV series (Winfrey 2013), shame can "creep into every corner and crevice of our lives."

We are not proposing that, as educators, we need to be therapists. But what we must do is understand the need for self-awareness and self-regulation. What are our responses when others fail to meet our expectations (adults and children alike), or we fail to meet our own? How alert are we to the *meaning* of the behaviors we see in children and young people in our schools, families, and the wider community? Some of these behaviors look very different through a trauma-informed lens, and we hope this chapter will alert you to some patterns of behavior that could well be defenses against the shame that is a result of a lifetime of adverse experiences rupturing the relationships that are critical to our healthy survival and development. A shame lens is part of our trauma lens.

In our buildings, classrooms, and school grounds, the conditions we create that maximize the positives of *interest and enjoyment* are inherently rewarding because they feel good and allow us to stay connected with our learners and them with their learning. We can work to minimize the conditions that trigger the negatives of *fear, anger, distress, disgust, contempt,* and *shame,* which are inherently punishing—they feel bad. They interfere with our connections with our learners and their families and, among our students, with each other. Our behaviors are rarely neutral—they are either connecting us or doing the opposite, disconnecting us. The challenge for us in writing about this is to simplify some complex messages; we hope this chapter can achieve this.

THE AFFECT SYSTEM

The limbic system (discussed in Chapter 3) is part of a complex system that alerts us to what information (sensory and interoceptive) needs *attention*: the information's degree of *salience*. If we could not identify what was important at the moment, we would suffer from sensory overload and be unable to respond in ways that improve the likelihood of survival—this is called stimulus confusion. A simple example of this affect system in action would be the capacity to concentrate on something that we are enjoying or deeply interested in, outweighing the sensory messages from our body about how uncomfortable the chair might be or whether we are too hot or cold or need a trip to the bathroom. We can put up with discomfort if what we are engaged with is more important than any physical discomfort we might be in right now.

This section refers to affect and script psychology,[1] the work of Silvan Tomkins, a psychologist, philosopher, and playwright who developed a theory of human behavior, motivation, and personality, best summarized by Silvan Tomkins and Virginia Demos in their book, *Exploring Affect: The Selected Writings of Silvan Tomkins* (Tomkins & Demos 1995). Most neuroscientists and psychologists would agree that the affect system is a complex network of neural pathways that, along with other core regulatory networks, connects the lower parts of the brain (brainstem) with the cortex, the thinking, rational part of the brain.

We only become consciously aware of a stimulus if it is sufficiently strong (salient) to trigger an affect, a neural response to the change in data. As explained in Chapter 3, any change in data is first processed in the lower parts of our brain before being processed again in the limbic system. These primary, innate neural responses (affects) are neither positive nor negative but serve as mechanisms to alert us to

---

[1]   Details of and the research around affect and script psychology can be found at www.tomkins.org.

these changes—to what is salient—and what to pay attention to now. When that happens, we become conscious of a negative or positive *feeling*. This is our *biology* at work. As our brain matures, we collect experiences (in patterns) stored in *implicit* memory (see Chapter 3). When these patterns are repeated through experience, this pattern and the associated memories become emotions. This is our *biography* at work. Over time, repetitions of these experiences, supported by memory, become *scripted* into the brain, helping us predict more efficiently (like a written script in a play tells the actor what comes next). It is the interaction of our cognitive (thinking, processing, and memory) systems and our affect system that can "more fully guarantee survival" (Kelly & Lamia 2018, p.11). This, of course, happens very quickly. For example, if our brainstem and amygdala have processed a visual stimulus, such as the look of anger on someone's face as a cue for danger, the response might be fight, flight, or freeze. Recall from Chapter 3 about brain basics, "Our brain is organized to act and feel before we think" (Perry & Winfrey 2021, p.29).

In Chapter 3, we mention how important predictability is to save the brain from learning everything anew every time a similar experience happens. Thus, a repeated angry facial expression and the implicit memory of what follows can predict danger. For a child or young person who has no way of identifying the feeling or its meaning or is even aware of it via their bodily responses (interoceptive data), it will be impossible for them to develop the capacity to self-regulate by using the influence of their higher-thinking cortex. This is just as true for adults. A wide enough vocabulary and a strong sense of what's happening in our bodies are both involved in self-regulation. Another issue here is that children, young people, and adults can misinterpret the facial expressions of others. The face (and its muscles) is the primary communication site, and these distinguishing facial expressions are clearer on young children's faces, less so on adult faces.

As adolescents, our kids (Marg) often thought I was angry about something when I was paying close attention, listening hard: "Why are you angry, Mum?" I would respond, "I'm not angry—this is my listening face!"

These affect mechanisms are present from birth. Once stimulated by brain activity, they provide the conditions that allow us to *pay attention* to what is important—what needs our attention. From the work of Abramson and Beck (2011), Abramson (2014), and Kelly and Lamia (2018), we can see the relationship between any affect that is triggered and *how it can motivate our own and others' behavior.* Understanding our own and others' behavior from the perspective of *emotional* motivation can help *us* stay regulated. Each affect has a distinguishing facial expression, seen best on babies' faces as they communicate with caregivers to increase the likelihood of survival when they are so vulnerable (see Table 8.1).

Table 8.1: Affect, motivation, and facial expression

Affect (as a continuum from mild to intense)	When triggered, it motivates us to	Facial expression (especially in very young children)
Interest—Excitement	Engage with the object, activity or person and stay engaged	Eyebrows down, eyes tracking, looking, listening
Enjoyment—Joy	Affiliate with the thing, activity, or person because it so rewarding	Smile, lips widened and out
Surprise—Startle	Stop. Look. Listen	Eyebrows up, blink
Shame—Humiliation	Seek to restore interrupted interest and/or enjoyment	Eyes down—loss of eye contact—head down, blush
Distress—Anguish	Signal the need to be soothed and comforted	Cry, rhythmic sobbing, arched eyebrows, mouth curved down
Anger—Rage	Attack (fight)	Frown, clenched jaw, red face
Fear—Terror	Run (flight)	Frozen stare, pale face, cold, sweaty
Disgust	Reject after sampling (get rid of). "You make me sick"	Lower lip out, head forward and down (as if about to spit the thing out)

cont.

Affect (as a continuum from mild to intense)	When triggered, it motivates us to	Facial expression (especially in very young children)
Dissmell[2]/Contempt	Reject before sampling (stay away) "I want nothing to do with you"	Upper lip raised; head pulled back (as if smelling something foul)

Adapted from Abramson (2014); Kelly and Lamia (2018).

As we develop and socialize, we learn to mask these facial responses to reduce our vulnerability, to *save face*, or to keep *a stiff upper lip*. We learn how to express our feelings verbally or non-verbally, or not at all, depending on how we were raised. Learning to read another's facial expression is a complex task, made more difficult by cultural differences and some special and diverse needs; for example, eye contact, so important in connections, is difficult for some children and adults who are on the autism spectrum. In some cultures, eye contact (from child to adult) is considered disrespectful. Reading facial expressions accurately is vital in developing social skills, which is more complex when culture and upbringing mask the basics. Kelly and Lamia (2018) and McShane (2020) show photos of facial expressions that are clearer and more recognizable on the faces of babies, children, and young people before they have learned to mask expressions to minimize vulnerability and adhere to cultural norms. On top of this, once we achieve adulthood, facial expression is often a *combination* of affects—another complication!

It is not simply that this understanding can explain all that we see in our own or others' behaviors. Our *history* of relationships and experiences in our families of origin, schools, communities, ethnicity, culture, and adverse childhood experiences will determine how we respond. It's a mix of our biology *and* biography. Self-regulation can only be acquired when we know ourselves well enough to know what is happening. As adults, if we use curiosity rather than judgment to discover what might be going on emotionally in ourselves, our students, and our colleagues, it will help us better to understand the behavior. The contingency programs of behaviorism involving

---

2   Dissmell (our physiological response to foul smells) is considered the biological basis for prejudice—rejection before sampling.

rewards and punishments so popular in many schools are woefully inadequate for recognizing shame and trauma-related behaviors— our own and our students' (more about this later in the chapter).

Our well-being depends on our capacity to maximize our positive experiences, minimize our negative experiences, communicate effectively about how we feel about what's happening to us, and how to do more of that more often. Teaching the children and young people in our schools about managing the challenge of balancing positive and negative feelings in healthy ways is a vital aspect of our formal and informal curriculum. *How we manage our relationships with them is critical.* Knowing ourselves first is necessary for managing our responses when our buttons are pushed.

SHAME

Turning our attention to the specifics of shame, the focus of this chapter, we might explain it as an "inbuilt social alarm" (Hansberry 2016, p.11). Given our biology as warm-blooded, hairy mammals who have evolved to live in community rather than in isolation, it makes good sense to have a mechanism that will alert us to an interruption of something that is a source of interest and enjoyment to us, or more simply, a disconnection—that something is amiss. Once this social alarm of shame-humiliation is triggered in our affect system, we become aware of a range of feelings and emotions, none of which is pleasant. That is the point, really—to pay attention to the cause of the impediment, so something might be done to remedy the situation.

In most of our Western cultures, we have a limited understanding of the biology of shame other than knowing that it feels bad and ought to be dispensed with as quickly as possible. It usually means "You should be ashamed of yourself" or "Shame on you." Tomkins and Demos (1995), Demos (2019), and Nathanson (1992) describe the conditions that might trigger shame: when there is a rupture (disconnection) of some sort in a relationship/connection, there is an interruption of the positive affects of interest and enjoyment. Shame results in a *family* of feelings, emotions, and behaviors. Brené Brown references some members of this family as "shame, guilt, humiliation and embarrassment" in her book *Atlas of the Heart* (2021, p.134). If we have been taught that shame is inherently bad, we learn to cope in unhelpful ways.

Therapist and colleague Joe Izzo, who works with war veterans suffering from PTSD in Washington, DC, is clear that the hardest shame to deal with from a therapeutic perspective is the shame because of a sense of helplessness felt when *freeze* is triggered in the brainstem in overwhelming situations. Being mobilized into fight or flight as part of a sympathetic response is "less shaming" (personal communication, December 11, 2022). In applying this thinking to our student population, there will be instances of freeze and immobilization that our young people have encountered when faced with an overwhelming threat, and they suffer the same kind of helplessness that triggers shame.

Shame is universal in humans. What is experienced as shameful or shaming will be very much determined by cultural norms. In Table 8.2, we have created examples of situations that could trigger shame (certainly in many Western cultures) and how that might be expressed verbally.

Table 8.2: How shame triggers might work

Interest and enjoyment in connecting	Situations that could cause impediment to positive affect	Examples of how "shame" might be expressed— "I feel..."
Friendship in a group	Harmful gossip about me	Hurt, helpless
New topic in class	Too hard to understand	Stupid and confused
A new partner	Being dumped	There's something wrong with me
Physical appearance	Acne and spots	Ugly and unlovable
Belonging in the group	Being singled out for public praise	Embarrassed
Racial pride	Racist remarks	Diminished, hurt
New laptop	New software is harder to understand	Frustrated, stupid
A planned visit from a friend	Doesn't show up	Disappointed, hurt, let down
Learning to play a new instrument	Harder than expected	Incompetent

Adapted from Kelly and Lamia (2018).

BIOLOGICAL RESPONSES TO SHAME

There are three significant biological responses, first noted by Charles Darwin (1873) in his *The Expression of the Emotions in Man and Animals*, when the shame of disconnection (or an interruption of interest and enjoyment) is triggered:

- *Blush:* We blush in situations where our social identity is threatened, when we are being scrutinized, when we are being overpraised, or when we are being told we are blushing even when we aren't! It is a central aspect of the regulation of social behavior. It is an autonomic (sympathetic) response triggered when we know others are watching us, perhaps knowing we have violated some rules or norms. This may trigger empathy in others (Cozolino 2014). Sadly, there is nothing much we can do to prevent it, and to be sure, sometimes the fact that we are blushing makes us feel more shame because there is no hiding it.

- *Loss of eye contact:* Head down, shoulders hunched, neck muscles go limp—this response is related to not wanting to be seen and judged, feeling exposed and vulnerable, a submissive behavior that has been conserved through our evolution. (Cozolino 2014). The very worst we can demand of a child or young person is to say, "Look at me when I'm speaking to you." With effective restorative responses, eye contact will be resumed when the student feels safe and free of judgment, when our response has been curious, not furious, and is empathic. We must also be aware of cultural differences in eye contact.

- *Cognitive shock:* Temporary cortical shutdown (or paralysis) is a significant response to intense feelings of shame when our capacity to think clearly at that moment is impeded, and we feel confused and flustered. This is a significant issue for learners in classrooms who are already dysregulated because there is little "broadband" available for learning and even less so when shamed. A significant decline/decay in cortical function occurs when too much stress/trauma is processed in the brain's lower parts. Dr. Bruce Perry refers to this when describing state-dependent functioning, and we write about this in detail in Chapter 3. He describes a sequence for a successful interaction between adult and child that starts with ensuring that both parties are *regulated* (therefore allowing better access to the cortex), then moves to connecting before correcting (*relating*, feeling safe), and only then does it become possible to *reason* (Perry & Szalavitz 2017).

The English language is rich in "emotion/feeling" words, which, to the shame-aware, would indicate that the *affect* of shame has been triggered due to a disconnection. Psychiatrist Don Nathanson, at an international conference presentation in Fort Worth, Texas, in 2010,[3] shared some of this language, suggesting a range of emotions that would have a basis in shame: embarrassed, exposed, dishonored, mortified, ruined, awkward, shy, abused, humbled, belittled, insulted, diminished, loss of face, rejected, humiliated, disrespected, ridiculed, excluded, patronized.

Other familiar words in common use, especially by us as educators and parents, might include disappointed, frustrated, alienated, rejected, abandoned, isolated, confused, inadequate, flawed, hurt, worthless, stupid, and judged.

Different languages also have words and meanings for shame. In Māori, the word is *whakamā*. Tanui Stephens (2020) writes in his opinion piece for *The Spinoff*:

> Whakamā is a major dynamic in the Māori world. Like the associated values of manaaki, utu and aroha it refers to our private and public connections with each other. It comes with a conscience.
>
> We suffer whakamā if we can't get to a tangi or iwi event. We are shamed if we cannot feed our visitors or offer the right speech or song. Stigma sticks if we let someone down. We must fulfil the cultural and humanist obligations that make us feel good about being Māori.
>
> Whakamā is not guilt for something you did, but humiliation for who you are. It's a deep hit to the core of your being. You are inferior, disgraced, disadvantaged: and you know it. It has an acute memory.
>
> Whakamā compels you to atone: to be 'at one' with the consequences

---

3   Recordings of this conference are available from www.tomkins.org.

of your actions. Whakamā is a clue that something stupid or bad has gone down and you need to fix it.

Throughout history, shame—the fear of it and the fact of it—has been a powerful corrective of human behavior. To actually feel shame requires personal humility and the acceptance of the value of other people. They have a right to exist and their opinions count. Whakamā stops us misbehaving and is one route to balance in society.

In Australia, the word *shame* in indigenous cultures signifies what may be felt when one is the center of attention, when receiving praise, when meeting strangers, in the presence of close relatives, when passing near a forbidden place, or when exposed to secret ceremony information. Most commonly, shame in Aboriginal culture includes a fear of negative consequences arising from perceived wrongdoing and disapproval and a strong desire to escape unpleasant situations (Harkins 1990).

In Japan and some other East Asian countries, there are words that, in the West, we would associate with shame—*haji* (meaning shame or embarrassment) and *hazukashii*. The latter is used with personal bad things that one does not want other people to know or see and is used by the caregiver, meaning shameful, ashamed, shy, or embarrassed, to call their children's attention to behaviors that have been negatively assessed by their caregivers, to develop empathy and compassion for others and comply with the social norms of the community. In his journal article for *New Voices in Japanese Studies*, Gian Marco Farese (2016) writes:

> In both cases, the bad feeling seems to derive from the fear that one's actions may be in contrast with social norms which are context-specific. If this is the case, this will attract people's criticism, and produce consequent effects that might include damage to the actor's reputation.

In commenting on honor/shame dynamics in Sub-Saharan Africa, Sandra Freeman (2015) writes that the culture is both shame-based and fear-based, that shame and fear are two sides of the same coin, and that it is *impossible* to have one without the other. The ancestors have left the elders as guardians of the tribal values. In this context, these values are not to be questioned, and community members live to avoid dishonoring and angering the ancestors and thus shaming the elders. This translates directly to fear of bringing shame to one's family in the eyes of the elders, the village, and the tribe. Freeman comments that collectivistic cultures train their members from birth to need the approval and acceptance of those around them and to draw their identity from how well they "fit" and belong to the group. She adds that this is achieved by applying the mechanism of honor/ shame and the fear of dishonoring their ancestors.

In all cultures, shame is a powerful social regulator, teaching us what to do and not do if we wish to stay connected with others. As humans, we are neurobiologically wired for this. Our culture and experiences teach us what is shameful and what is not. Shame is neither good nor bad. It is simply information designed to motivate us to do something to restore us to what was good—to reconnect after a disconnection, to repair the ruptures that have occurred. Biologically, shame is restoratively motivational.

The issue with this data that shame provides is that it is inherently punishing, so we pay attention to it. Once triggered into our consciousness, the feeling can produce more shame, especially if we draw painful conclusions about ourselves through life experiences. Brené Brown perfectly sums up this second wave of shame as "the intensely painful feeling or experience of believing that we are flawed and therefore unworthy of love, belonging, and connection" (2021, p.137). This feeling is so painful that we have developed an array of behaviors to defend ourselves against it and push it away. Hansberry (2016) advises:

> ...to hang in there with the moment of shame, and then follow through with self-reflection and social reconnection, we must feel as though we are loved and accepted by others... The problem is that in the moment of shame we may feel terribly exposed, so utterly defective, that it is easy to forget that there is anything good about us—anything worthy of pride... When shame strikes and we don't feel loved and accepted, we are completely helpless to do anything constructive with shame. (p.97)

Aside from understanding the biology of shame, the clear message here is that, as educators, we need to have enough cultural awareness to minimize the chance of unnecessarily shaming others.

When we think about raising our children and teaching others' children in our schools, we use the social regulation aspect of shame (pointing out the wrongness of behavior) to help develop an *internal locus of control*—self-regulation—to stay within the norms. Others might call this a *moral compass*. The disapproval of an adult or group who matters to us is *shaming* and must be followed by a process of reconnection and reintegration for the shame to be discharged (e.g., the disapproval of something done at home must be followed by an act of reconnection such as a hug; in a school, a "telling off" must be followed by a check-in to ensure the rupture is healed—"Are we okay now?"). The deed must be differentiated from the doer for this to happen. Punitive consequences cannot achieve this outcome, but restorative approaches, done well, can allow reconnection after a disconnection.

SHAME AND SCHOOL DISCIPLINE POLICIES

We have mentioned in Chapter 2 the limited capacity of behaviorism to develop a moral compass and enhance self-regulation in children and young people. Let's remind ourselves here that what we observe in the behavior of others is merely the outward visible sign of what we can't see happening inside the brain.

There is still a heavy reliance on punitive, archaic responses to achieve compliance: corporal punishment in some states and countries, suspensions (stand-downs and fixed-term exclusions) and exclusions, zero tolerance, detentions, time out, banning students from participating in field trips, public humiliation—the list is endless. These responses often reflect the community's expectations about how schools should respond to wrongdoing and a lack of understanding about what *really* works (Thorsborne & Vinegrad 2022). When we were reading recently about proposed legislation in Canada to change Section 43 of the Canadian criminal code (to outlaw the use of violence against children), it was astonishing to see how many responses on social media support the use of physical violence to teach "respect," with many comments echoing the viewpoint "It taught me to be respectful" or "It's bad if it's a beating, but okay if it's a smack" and "It didn't do me any harm." What this *does* teach is *compliance*, with little understanding of the meaning of respect. Never mind that violence against *adults* is a crime, and violence against children is not.

These views are deeply entrenched in a significant proportion of our population, no matter what country, and very hard to shift; the science–practice gap—an average of 17 years—is mostly related to the medical field of research-into-practice (Munro & Savel 2016). We know from our decades of immersion in schools that this gap also exists around how long new approaches will take to catch up to the research, especially with brain development and the impact of trauma on behavior.

When we think about using punishment (blaming and shaming) to teach compliance, traditional practice banishes the student temporarily or permanently from the class or school, casting them out of the herd. Tim Brighouse and Mick Waters (2021), in their (literally) huge book about the state of schools in the UK, lament the overuse of fixed-term (suspensions) and permanent exclusions, especially for boys, which tend to lead them straight into the criminal justice system (the school-to-prison pipeline). They write that this policy has been catastrophic.

How does this deliberate shaming help the development of skills we mention in Chapter 2—empathy and honesty? How does it encourage the development of awareness of how the behavior has impacted others? How does this improve the likelihood that we are helping this young person develop conflict competence and perspective-taking? How does this reconnect all those involved in the problem, heal the harm, and rebuild the affected community? How do these behavioristic approaches build the skills that are absent from the child's repertoire, especially when the skills they do have served a purpose at some stage but are not acceptable in the school community?

If we view these practices through a shame and blame lens, *this* form of social regulation fails to separate the deed from the doer and risks the development of "I'm a bad person" rather than "I've done a bad thing." Emeritus Professor John Braithwaite (1989), now-retired criminologist, highly respected researcher, and author, writes about *stigmatizing* shaming and its limited positive impact on changing the trajectory of those involved in the criminal justice system, suggesting that reintegrative processes will be much more effective in building safer communities and reducing re-offending. Dr. Vick Kelly (2014a), a psychiatrist and therapist, writes:

To minimize people by treating them as if all they are is their behavior is to misunderstand the essence of what makes us human. Punitive methods of dealing with detrimental behaviors are destined to fail because they dehumanize the person, creating more shame and harm in people whose behaviors most likely stem from the fact that they are already harmed. (p.52)

None of these standard punitive responses consider our biology, or more specifically, our neurobiology, or an understanding of the impact of trauma. Lori Desautels and Michael McKnight (2019), in support of these views, write:

The majority of our schools use the term "consequences" rather than "punishments," but in effect they are often one and the same. They are meant to cause some form of pain to teach the child a lesson. The vast majority of the time they are used over and over again with children and youth who have experienced trauma and neglect and are already in pain… It is time to move beyond the simplistic and traditional view of rewarding and punishing good behaviour. (pp.76–77)

While we have limited our discussion here to responses around inappropriate behavior, it might be useful to consider the role of shame in learning, since much shame is generated in the struggles with learning. Some children would rather be seen as stupid, naughty, or the class clown than let a teacher or their classmates know they are not coping. Graeme George (2014) writes about the confusion a student might experience in attempting to learn new work:

In that moment of confusion, of cognitive shock, the student may attribute the block to one of two causes…not thinking clearly enough or deeply enough…or to some deficiency in the self that will make it impossible ever to grasp this concept. (p.219)

Widening our lens to a broader view of the current pervasive culture of shaming, particularly in the West—anyone who does not "fit" our ideas of being fully human (men, women, the mentally ill, poor, gay, transgender, people of color, political and religious affiliations, disability and so on)—we can also predict that these beliefs will have a hugely detrimental impact on the developing brain of a child who identifies with any of these groups, and these may lie unchallenged in our systems, policies, and practices. It is not possible in the scope of this book to detail how this happens. Vick Kelly writes in a personal communication (2022, September 25) via email:

> It's likely whole books could and should be written about the issue of group shaming. This is especially true because...one must look closely at those who do the shaming to understand their motivation. In what way are their actions a response to the needs of their central blueprint? How do their attitudes and beliefs become scripted? What are the biopsychosocial determinants behind the behaviors? Why do some members of a community/culture that shames a particular group not engage in those behaviors/beliefs?

So, how do we shift a child's thinking about a flawed self and give them hope for a different future?

SHAME PATTERNS AND TRAUMA

This idea that one may draw a conclusion about oneself when shame has been triggered is the perfect segue to understanding the crippling effect of shame when we are exposed to situations over which we have very little control. Psychiatrist Paul Conti, a guest on the Huberman Lab podcast (Huberman 2022), defines trauma as something that overwhelms our coping skills and leaves us different. It changes our brain function, and these changes become evident as we move forward through life.

This helplessness and hopelessness, if repeated often enough, give rise to patterns of responses (scripts) that help us make sense of what's happening, predict likely outcomes, and increase our capacity to survive (Kelly 2014b). Many of these response patterns were necessary when faced with adverse childhood experiences. Still, unless challenged with care, love, and patience, they show up in the behaviors we find so frustrating in our schools and classrooms. When (although not always) the threats no longer exist, these responses become maladaptive in the modern world.

There are many situations in which the child has absolutely no control (issues like abuse, neglect, chaos, poverty, housing and food security, discrimination, bias, and prejudice) to change the outcome for themselves and to become reconnected to caregivers, the group, or the community. When this happens, the information that shame provides cannot be used constructively, so the child develops defenses to protect themselves from the unbearable pain of disconnection. In his book *Shame and Pride*, Don Nathanson (1992) developed a framework to understand these families of defense responses against shame. It is known in affect and script psychology circles as the "Compass of Shame" (see Figure 8.1) and describes patterns of responses that have become stable over time (scripts).

I (Marg) can never read, write about, or share this model without better understanding myself and how I default at the moment—how my "scripts" work. It may take me days to figure out why I feel so bad about myself, and when I do, the "aha" moment is such a relief because I can then figure out what to do about it! It also allows me to be curious about the underlying behaviors I see and experience in myself and others. Oh, and how I might self-regulate and help others do the same!

COMPASS OF SHAME

There are four poles in the Compass of Shame (see Figure 8.1). Each of the poles in this diagram represents a family of behaviors that can be deeply scripted into our brains if the shame we experience is too painful and chronic. Withdrawal and avoidance represent *flight* from shame, and attack self and attack other could be understood as *fighting* with shame.

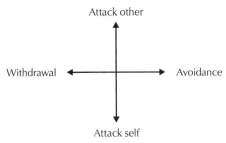

Figure 8.1: Compass of Shame
ADAPTED FROM DON NATHANSON (1992).

Withdrawal pole

We pull away from people and experiences that do or might cause shame. We anticipate/predict further shame, so we go into hiding. The risk of exposure, of being seen as defective, is too great. This hiding can be literal (walking home instead of catching the bus for fear of being teased), retreating to our room, or refusing to participate in social activities for fear of rejection. It can silence our voice in a classroom or group if we make mistakes and are laughed at. It makes perfect sense when we look at this response through the lens of the autonomic nervous system and its dorsal vagal response of freeze (Dana 2020)! The threat of further shame-humiliation means we pull away.

Avoidance pole

This involves behaviors that attempt to remove the feelings of shame from our consciousness. In other words, we are hiding these unbearable feelings from ourselves—we are *in denial*. Many enjoy a cold beer on a hot day or a fine wine with dinner with friends. Still, when using alcohol, other drugs, and prescription medications to stop these feelings and thoughts about our imperfections, self-medication can become a pattern of addiction. These strategies keep us from connecting with others, which means our world of connection with others is at risk. There are many ways in which we can pretend to ourselves that we are okay: obsessively spending too much money on "stuff," perfectionism (I'm only loveable if I'm perfect), the pursuit and accumulation of wealth (a better house, car, boat, to "keep up with the Joneses"), needing to win at all costs, the posting of images on social media to send a message about what we have, where we are going, who we are with, so our followers will think better of us.

We have come to understand that young people who seem incapable of telling the truth about their involvement in an incident of harm or a breach of the rules and norms manage the possible humiliating and frightening fallout of taking responsibility. To develop a student's willingness to tell the truth, we must consider several factors: how safe they feel to "fess up," how they might be punished at home for bringing shame on their families, and where honesty fits in their culture.

How about their parents' responses? We often speak of parents being overly defensive or adversarial when we call or invite them to the school to discuss their child's behaviors. This situation often triggers absolute denial: "My child would never do that," "This surely must be the teacher's fault," or "That is the other child's fault." Perhaps what's going on for them is a response to their shame. It's for good reason that this point on the Compass of Shame is often called the pole of denial.

Attack self pole

It seems odd that beating oneself up can make us feel better. It works like this: if I get in first and blame myself, I can control and lessen the likelihood of any possible attack and blame from others.

I (Marg) am trying to wean myself off this particular habit of attack self when I catch up with someone I haven't seen for ages. If they comment positively about how well I look, my standard response is always to put myself down. Yes, I say, I am well, but as I get older, my waistline increases. Heaven forbid this person has a crack at me for looking fatter than the last time we caught up! It is better for me to criticize than for them to do that, which I would find unbearable. I suspect this is a script developed in childhood in my attempts to handle how social regulation strategies used by my parents impacted me as a child!

We often hear students wrestling with the confusion (shame) they feel when struggling with their learning: "I'm dumb, I'm stupid, I'm a loser." Attack self can develop into more serious forms such as self-harm (e.g., patterns of cutting, burning, putting ourselves in harm's way) and the ultimate attack on self, suicide. Remember Brené Brown's definition of the impact of shame: "The intensely painful feeling or experience of believing that we are flawed and therefore unworthy of love, belonging, and connection" (Brown 2021, p.137). How very sad that a person can no longer bear these feelings about themselves and see the future as utterly hopeless or believe they don't deserve to live—that the world would be a better place if they did not inhabit it.

Attack other pole

This script manifests in our need to feel better about ourselves by making others feel worse. This is a cheat's way to self-esteem, what we see in this behavior in ourselves and others. It can range from put-downs, sarcasm, verbal abuse—any abuse for that matter—bullying, physical violence, road rage, family violence, social media trolling, and eventually, in the worst case, murder. These behaviors shift attention away from us and onto others. It's the blame game happening—it's YOUR fault. You deserve to be punished. It may escalate to revenge, payback, tit-for-tat, and retribution—characteristics of punitive policies in our schools, some families, and the wider community, especially in the criminal justice system. It might manifest itself in a classroom where behavior is difficult to manage, and the teacher feels that he is no longer in control and, therefore, incompetent. His response is angry and abusive, publicly humiliating the student in front of other learners. No wonder we might see an equivalent "attack other" response from the student that might take the form of swearing, drawing attention to the teacher's physical appearance or sexual orientation (whether known or not) and how hopeless a teacher they are. When we consider these shame-defensive behaviors of adults at home, it is easy to see how some of these patterns may show up in children's school behaviors.

Many of these feelings can be masked by anger—anger pro-duces a great deal of adrenaline, mobilizing us to face the danger of humiliation, and it sure feels better than shame. If we are not careful, we miss the opportunity to explore what lies beneath and end up matching that anger with anger and escalating the situation. We are on a "hiding to nowhere" (a hopeless endeavor) with this shame-rage spiral if we are seeking to find a solution. One of the best, immediate options when facing this situation is to self-regu-late and then help the student self-regulate (co-regulation in action) until the adrenaline surge has settled to a state of parasympathetic calmness, allowing us to connect (relate) and then begin a relational, problem-solving dialogue (reason). Enabling young people to name the affect/feeling/emotion and describe how their body reacts can be very helpful. Taking responsibility for any part we might have played in escalating the situation will also help.

When we view this response to shame through the lens of the impact of trauma on the developing brain, we can better understand the likelihood of the script formation of *I am imperfect, ugly, unworthy, defective, undeserving, and incompetent*. This knowledge helps us understand how those traumatized respond, to be protective, shame - and fear-reducing, but not helping to reconnect with self and others.

HOW RESTORATIVE HELPS

If we, as adults, are attuned to our feelings and behaviors in such a way that we can self-regulate, we can begin to explore what happened in an incident by being curious, not furious; by being prepared to explore rather than explode; to understand before having our concerns understood. It is *not* about making excuses for the behavior or letting the child off the hook, but rather viewing the behavior through a trauma-informed and shame-sensitive lens.

If we respond with empathy to the stories of both those harmed and those responsible, the sting of shame can be metabolized by the interest of others, free of judgment, in our stories. Shame can morph into guilt for those responsible, a healthier version that allows us to move from beating ourselves or others up in the blame game to safely escaping denial and withdrawal. Shame can then do its job to motivate us to make things right and restore ourselves and our connections with others. We are separating the deed from the person, understanding how "it" happened. What harm was the result? Asking those in the problem to collaborate as a community to find solutions built on a shared understanding. To reconnect after a disconnection. Is this not restorative practice in action?

This chapter has been longer than most in this book, and we are grateful that you have stayed the distance because the links between shame and trauma are well known. This knowledge will help us to think differently about ourselves and others when disconnections occur, and this will allow us to make better decisions.

CENTRAL IDEAS

★ Shame accompanies trauma, and we need to recognize it when it is triggered in ourselves and accurately interpret its symptoms in the behaviors of our students, parents, caregivers, and colleagues.

★ Self-awareness around what triggers our thoughts and feelings around shame and other emotions is central to self-regulation if we are to help others regulate.

★ Shame can be regarded as a social alarm informing us that a disconnection needs attention, which is important to survival as social animals.

★ Affects and emotions play a significant role in motivating our behavior.

★ Our well-being depends on our capacity to balance the positive and negative aspects of our lives and the lives of our students in healthy ways.

★ The experience of shame is powerful, and we need to diminish it quickly. If we don't know how to do that in healthy ways, our defenses against shame can make matters worse.

★ Shame is universal in humans, but what is shaming and shameful is determined by culture.

★ The physiology of shame is universal: loss of eye contact, blushing, and cognitive shock.

★ Shame is a form of social regulation in child rearing and teaching acceptable behaviors.

★ Using deliberate shaming in school policy and practice to improve compliance does not develop new pro-social skills; it does more harm.

★ This kind of deliberate shaming increases the likelihood of developing anti-social skills as young people try to minimize the impact of shame on how they view themselves.

★ Deliberate shaming does more harm to students already harmed by their traumatic experiences.

★ Shame defense behaviors can be organized into families of behaviors described in the Compass of Shame: withdrawal, avoidance (denial), attack self, attack other.

★ Effective and skilled facilitation of restorative processes allows participants to discharge their shame and reconnect after disconnection.

REFLECTIVE QUESTIONS

✓ What were your earliest remembered experiences of disapproval of a significant adult in your life? What conclusions did you reach about yourself? Where did you feel it in your body? Now, as an adult, where do you feel it? How are those early memories of shame shaping what happens to you in the now?

✓ If you have suffered significant trauma, does understanding shame's biology bring some relief? Were you allowed to make things right, moving away from the shame of being "less than" into guilt about what you had done? If you were punished for your mistake, did the punishment itself motivate you to put it right, or rather to be compliant?

✓ When you think about your approaches in your classroom, do you have a sense of whether the strategies you use might trigger shame or minimize the likelihood that shame will be triggered?

✓ What is your pattern of shame defense when you have bungled and disconnected in some way or been shamed by another?

✓ What do you notice about how your students handle their shame?

✓ What do you better understand now about how parents may react to negative feedback about their children?

✓ What might be a better response to someone else's shame and defensiveness?

In our final chapter, we hope to bring everything together in a coherent understanding of the personal, professional, and social journey that we embark on when we become educators.

— CHAPTER 9 —

Becoming a Trauma-Informed Restorative Educator: Pulling it All Together

When we set out to write this book, we had no idea about the journey we had committed ourselves to and the challenge it represented—the advantage of not knowing what we did not know and how hard it would be! We knew this material was vitally important in the changing world of classrooms and education, particularly in the wake of the pandemic, the loss of trust in our institutions, and the changes wrought socially by the overreliance on our devices to connect and communicate. We did not realize the richness and speed of the changing knowledge about our brains.

As explained in our Introduction, the work we must do is a journey along three pathways—personal, professional, and social justice. They are completely intertwined. We cannot hope to address our classroom culture, school policy, and practice without first understanding what is going on in our brains—our own brain state and how stressed we are—and knowing what to do now to help regulate ourselves before others.

This is the first path—our personal journey—at work, home, the shopping plaza, or attending our children's competitive sporting matches. We hope that, at this point in the book, you are beginning to see that this personal journey is about knowing and befriending your own nervous system and all the things that come with that, like owning your emotions and the events that activate you. It means taking control of your wellness beyond self-care and moving to living a regulated life by paying attention to the things that dysregulate us, like poor nutrition, poor sleep, or lack of movement for our bodies. It also means building a network of humans that offer us relational wealth. Spending time with these people fills our emotional buckets.

Our personal journey is a shift in how we see the behavior of others, moving away from this lens of manipulative children to one of struggling children who have undeveloped brains and lots of moments of dysregulation. It is hard to unsee from this lens once we have it. The world changes, compassion grows, and we find better ways to be the better versions of ourselves.

We need to keep up with our personal journey because it is a way for us to heal ourselves and create the space for others to heal. We need to keep reading the science and attend workshops and conferences. We are responsible for our own journey, our own learning, and our own healing!

Our second path—the professional journey—is when we bring the paradigm shift we arrived at through our personal work into our professional lives. It means we must examine our practices, structures, routines, and pedagogy so our classroom has more cues of safety than threat. It requires us to take a second glance at our classroom environments to ensure we account for children's sensory needs. We also need to make sure we see behavior as a result of nervous system states, not poor choices. This new lens also requires us to ask, "What experiences does this child need to have to develop the skills they need to manage their behavior?" This new question will replace the outdated question, "What consequence does this child need?"

Last is our social justice journey. What biases do we have hiding in plain sight, and what are we doing to change our biases? How does bias show up in our classroom from us or others? Do we know how to connect in truly relational (restorative) ways when dealing with behaviors in classrooms, corridors, and the schoolyard without relying on old, outdated ways of developing collaboration and co-operation based on command and control? This path challenges our old beliefs about what we have taken for granted for decades, the theories that underpin the behavioral science space. These theories are built on assumptions that behavior is only changed by manipulating the external environment—"Do this and you'll get that!" Incentives and sanctions have seeped so deeply into school culture that our feathers become ruffled when these ideas are refuted and challenged by the fresh research by neuro- and social scientists.

What is the lens we use when we think about the wider school community, its culture (how we do things around here), and the commitment we have, as individuals or as a whole school, to the third path, the social justice journey? How is it that we are promoting, in the words of Kathy Evans and Dorothy Vaandering in their *Little Book of Restorative Justice in Education* (2022, p.58), just and equitable relationships in our schools where "everyone is treated with worth and dignity, regardless of their race, ethnicity, religion, nationality, ability, economic class, language, body type, gender or sexual orientation."

Evans and Vaandering also point to Maslow's work around meeting our hierarchy of needs and the conclusions of Ryan and Deci's self-determination theory and intrinsic, self-directed motivation (Ryan & Deci 2020). Unsurprisingly, they also mention Howard Zehr (1990, 2015), who articulates core autonomy, trust, and relatedness needs. Humanistic ideals are based on human needs, not behaviorism and behavior modification.

Neuroscience has made it clear that for us as adults to thrive, we first need to feel safe, and we know that a felt sense of safety is critical for our learners, along with a genuine sense that they matter to us and each other. This science also tells us what we need to feel connected to thrive and to be well in our bodies, brains, and relationships. Not all of us have been afforded that sense of well-being in our own life history and circumstances. We know better now what it takes to achieve this, to heal ourselves and our relationships, and we can extend these lessons into the small things we do in our practice in classrooms, policies, and systems.

A CALL TO ACTION

Our call to action is for this book to become a vehicle for some tough discussions about how education is done. It is a call to action to make changes for ourselves, our classrooms, and our communities. To support those conversations, we have created an inventory summarizing the territory we have traversed together in this book (see Table 9.1). It is a discussion tool, not a checklist. You will find it at the end of this chapter and in the appendices. We encourage you to travel on this journey with a colleague or two, possibly creating a professional book club at your school, team, or faculty. Take your time to poke about the inventory here after you have read part or all of the book. Make up more questions! Discuss your three journeys by column or row. See where it takes you. There will be times when you are challenged and others when you are reassured (you always knew but did not have the words). Sometimes, you may be temporarily undone by what you have read—you may need some professional help to settle.

Keep reading. Science continues to change. Who knows what we will know in five or ten years?

Enjoy the rich satisfaction of the experiences ahead of you as you experiment with new ways of doing business with yourself, your students, parents, and colleagues and how this might change the culture in your classroom and, in the end, the school. We must move beyond old, outdated ideas about what drives behavior and embrace the latest that neuroscience has to offer so that we can give our children and young people the best opportunity to become their best selves.

We hope this journey creates a better world for all of us.

Table 9.1: Personal, professional and social justice journey inventory

What I have come to understand in my...	Personal journey? What do I realize?	Professional journey? What would be noticed?	Social justice journey? What would be noticed?
Theories and mindsets about behavior and motivation	What aspects of my practice have been informed by behavioral science?	How does behaviorism show up in my classroom?	How does behaviorism show up in school policy and practices?
Intrinsic motivation conditions (i.e., autonomy, competence, and relatedness)	What aspects of how I go about the work I do reflect these three conditions? How does it feel for me?	How am I building these conditions into my planning and delivery? How are students reacting to my encouragement of self-directed motivation?	What larger projects are developing these conditions across the school population? How am I helping?

The basics of brain structure and function	What has happened to me and my brain during my life? What is happening now?	What do I better understand about brain development in children and adolescents?	What do injustice, inequity, and discrimination do to the way brains develop and function? What am I seeing?
Fight, flight, or freeze behaviors	What responses of my own show up in my stress responses? Am I aware of my own activators?	What am I now seeing in individual and classroom behaviors that I can better understand through brain science?	Through the lens of school policy and practice, how does the school view and respond to fight, fight, or freeze behaviors?
Becoming aware of triggers that influence behavior	What makes me feel safe or unsafe?	What do I see affecting a sense of safety for my students? How do I know when they feel safe or unsafe?	What issues in general trigger whole-school community dysregulation?
My nervous system has cues that activate it	What do students do that activates my system? Can I work on those responses?	What sorts of issues in my classroom activate students' nervous systems?	What recent specific issues and/or incidents have caused upheaval?
My nervous system state is contagious	How am I staying regulated, so I have it to share?	How am I sharing my state? Is it positive or negative?	How am I offering calm to others in my community?
Implicit bias—hiding in plain sight	What have I discovered about myself and about the biases I have? How has this impacted my behavior and challenged my connections?	How does bias show up in my classroom? What feedback would my students offer me if I asked?	How does bias show up in my school's policy, especially around disciplinary matters?

cont.

What I have come to understand in my...	*Personal journey?* What do I realize?	*Professional journey?* What would be noticed?	*Social justice journey?* What would be noticed?
Relational approaches to problem-solving	Am I using a range of restorative options that reflect my understanding and commitment to humanistic approaches to relational education?	Am I working to connect my students with each other, promoting kindness and collaboration?	Has my school embarked on a path of culture change to develop awareness, change mindsets and practices that reflect the value of relationships? Am I contributing?
Connecting	Do I understand what really matters to my learners? Do they feel connected to me?	Do I greet and welcome my students at the door and find out how ready they are for learning?	Do I extend this relationship development work to my colleagues and the parents?
Modeling	Am I prepared to model the behaviors I want to see? Which of these do I need to develop?	Are my students starting to show how my modeling is having an impact?	Am I showing up in school meetings and professional development sessions willing to model these preferred behaviors? Do I speak up? Do I encourage the voice of others?
Regulating and co-regulating	Can I tell when I need to settle myself? I must regulate my own brain first.	Do I have routines in place that help individuals and the whole class to settle, ready for learning, and strategies to help those students who are still struggling?	Is our whole school committed to the ideas and practices of regulation and co-regulation? Is there is a coherent approach to achieving this? What would be seen?

Movement is regulating	Am I getting enough movement in the day to keep me regulated?	Are my students getting enough movement?	Are there regulating activities built into the school culture?
Attending to wellness	Am I paying attention to the needs of my body and brain health?	Am I aware of how healthy my relationships are with my colleagues? If unhealed ruptures exist involving me, am I prepared to work on them?	Is our whole school community characterized by trusting and mutually respectful relationships? Is this a key value that guides decisions?
Impact of trauma on the brain and behavior	Do I have a better understanding now of how stress and any trauma have impacted me?	Do I understand the backgrounds of my students so that I can view their behavior through a trauma-informed lens and respond in ways that settle and connect with them?	Does the school understand that trauma comes in all shapes and sizes; that its policies, practices, and structures can cause more harm? Is our school seeking to minimize these harms?
Understanding the impact of shame	What shames me? How do I respond when that happens?	How do I minimize unnecessary shame in my classroom? What behaviors of mine have I committed to changing?	Have we as a whole community identified the policies, structures, and practices that shame children and adults? Are we committed to minimizing the likelihood of intentionally shaming our community?

cont.

What I have come to understand in my...	*Personal journey?* What do I realize?	*Professional journey?* What would be noticed?	*Social justice journey?* What would be noticed?
The six elements of positive developmental and educational settings (the six Rs)	Do my lessons meet any of the six elements?	Are my students connecting to me as an educator? And to the lesson I am teaching?	Is respect the underlying space for my lessons?
This work is intentional	How am I setting myself up to be trauma-informed and restorative?	How am I setting up my classroom to be trauma-informed and restorative?	How am I intentionally addressing issues of injustice in my community?

Bal-A-Vis-X

It was a cold, blustery January day as I walked across campus from the coffee shop. I balanced the tray of coffee as I navigated my way up the steep steps to the old gym building. As I opened the door, my nervous system started to regulate as I heard the slow, steady rhythm of 60 racquetballs striking the floor in the same microsecond...patterned, repetitive, rhythmic movement. The synchronicity did not occur accidentally; it resulted from precise physical techniques that anyone could learn.

Bal-A-Vis-X is a series of **Bal**ance-Auditory-**Vis**ion-e**X**ercises of varied complexity that utilize beanbags, racquet balls, balance boards, and multiple principles and activities from educational kinesiology that require full-body coordination and focused attention. As a school-friendly activity, it demands cooperation and fosters peer teaching. Students who participate in Bal-A-Vis-X understand that once they learn an exercise, they do not become entitled; they become responsible for teaching the exercises to someone else.

I attended many Bal-A-Vis-X training sessions with the creator, Bill Hubert. Bill was a first-grade teacher in an urban midwestern school district in the United States. During his years of teaching, it seemed that each year he had three groups of students: one group that learned no matter how he taught them and sometimes despite him, another group that, with a little extra time and attention, usually began to show progress between Christmas and spring break, and a third group that, even with extra time, attention, and specialized learning never seemed to make adequate progress. He decided that he had to find another career if he couldn't help the third group of children; however, Bill also had a background in martial arts, which gave him a keen eye for physical movements. He knew he had to find a way to help them.

As Bill watched his first-graders through the lens of martial arts, he noticed a pattern; most students who made academic progress could also stand on one foot, jump off a chair and land on two feet, and use their bodies to swing and walk on a balance beam. He also noticed that most of the students who struggled to progress academically were those who struggled with physical tasks. Bal-A-Vis-X promotes self-challenge and is appropriate for nearly every student as it can:

- encourage cognitive integration

- settle a dysregulated nervous system

- decrease impulsivity and increase focus

- improve physical coordination.

As Bill began his journey to help his most struggling students, he heard through the grapevine about a nun facilitating a lab for struggling readers at a local university. He made an appointment to visit Sister Aegedia. She allowed him a short interview and a short tour when he arrived. "In a huge open area were kids of all ages crawling, rolling, climbing ropes and ladders, skipping, jumping rope, lying supine, watching a tennis ball (attached to twine) swing in circles, walking heel-to-toe on painted lines." He left the reading lab curious, and his journey to the present-day *Bal*ance-*A*uditory-*Vis*ion-e*X*ercises began over 30 years ago.

Bal-A-Vis-X is always evolving to meet the needs of the folks who will benefit the most. In the past ten years, the research of Dr. Bruce Perry, Dr. Bessel van der Kolk, and many others has led to the understanding that Bal-A-Vis-X supports the ideas of trauma-responsive care. Most Bal-A-Vis-X activities are deeply rooted in rhythm. The patterned, repetitive, rhythmic movement helps to calm the stress response. The many variations of the exercises provide opportunities to practice skills such as working memory, problem-solving, task initiation, and self-management, to name a few. The exercises start simple and become increasingly more challenging.

Bal-A-Vis-X movement and learning activities promote body/brain connection as they involve crossing the three midline planes of the body:

- *Sagittal plane:* Cuts the body into "left" and "right" halves. Involves forward and backward movements, such as tapping or stepping forward or backward, or a forward or backward lunge.

- *Frontal plane:* Cuts the body into front and back halves. Involves any lateral or side-to-side movement.

- *Transverse plane:* Cuts the body into top and bottom halves. Involves rotational movement such as twisting.

Bal-A-Vis-X activities cross the meridian (body's midline) in these three dimensions, at a steady rhythmic pace. The exercises are carefully modulated to become increasingly difficult or simplified for those with the most severe special needs. From a neurological perspective, these dimensions correlate with brain development in how it sequences activities, how the activities are interrelated, and how we develop coordination. These three dimensions of movement in the brain/body connection provide the basis for understanding how we grow and develop and how we can continue to change beyond our current capabilities at any age and within our current capabilities, meaning Bal-A-Vis-X is appropriate for any individual—even beyond the classroom.

I set down my tray of coffee as the exercise changed. The young person leading the group—yes, I said "young" person—gently stopped the exercise and began a new pattern. The 60 adults watched and joined precisely at the right moment to avoid interrupting synchronicity. I smiled as I listened to the bounce, catch, and clap because I knew this rhythmic synchronicity was more than possible, even with small children.

In my 15 years of teaching Bal-A-Vis-X to folks of all ages, I have never had one that couldn't learn the foundational exercises that can bring any human into a state of integration within just a few minutes. Over the years, I have seen folks benefit in many ways from the Bal-A-Vis-X exercises, but the one that means the most is the transformation of my son from an "I can't kid" to an "I can kid," and for that, I am forever grateful.

Contributor: Meagan Baldwin

Drumming in the Torres Strait

Drumming improves self-regulation and hearing at a primary/ elementary school campus for Indigenous students in the Torres Strait, a body of water separating the northernmost tip of Australia from Papua New Guinea. On Dauan, one of the many small islands in the Strait, is one of the elementary school campuses of Tagai State College; the college has 17 campuses spread across the islands. This account of what happens in the mornings before lessons start is from Ben Malpas, acting Head of Campus at this tiny school.

Each morning at school, we begin our day with a simple yet important routine. Every morning, we start with morning drumming. Students dance together to traditional songs accompanied by the beating of drums. The vigorous dancing helps to clear their nasal passages before completing a breath, cough, blow routine. Our students often present with hearing difficulties associated with congested inner, middle, and outer ears. This routine, with a high-quality microphone and speaker systems utilized by teachers to support their daily instructions, helps our students maintain their best hearing for the school day, and, with the drumming and dance, regulation of their bodies and brains.

The morning routine is strictly adhered to each day, providing students with predictable, rhythmic consistency, allowing them to turn in to class and settle. The drumming routine is followed by our school prayer, their student affirmation, and recital of our four school expectations, "proud learners who are respectful, responsible, and safe." This recital is completed in dual languages: Kala Kawaw Ya and standard Australian English.

Each year, our senior students take increased control of the drumming and the management of student behaviors in adhering to the routines, building trust through leadership. This establishes them as emerging elders.

Many of our teachers come from non-indigenous backgrounds and communities, and the senior students support their participation to build rapport between students and staff and foster an understanding of student backgrounds and cultures.

The morning drumming routine is also used to create a positive culture for learning, with the behavioral focus of the week being discussed with students to promote a genuine understanding of how campus expectations support their learning. Messages are delivered by all teachers and staff who work with the students, and students are encouraged to participate in these conversations about their understanding of expectations and to construct these expectations jointly.

After the morning routines, students are dismissed and accompanied by their teachers, who reinforce expectations and provide a structured learning transition.

Contributor: Ben Malpus

APPENDIX C

Yoga and "Weightless"

Lindy Anning works for the Department of Education in Queensland, Australia. She has taught in rural and remote areas, and in primary, high, and special schools in Central Queensland. On a training course for restorative practices, while we were exploring Bruce Perry's ideas of regulate, relate, and reason, she told a story about how she helped regulate a small class of students with a range of special needs. We have never forgotten her story and reached out to her for a written version to share in this book. What follows are the questions that were put to her about this story.

WHAT DID YOU NOTICE ABOUT THIS GROUP OF STUDENTS YOU WERE TEACHING?

It was a group of eight girls and boys between the ages of 11 and 15. The students all had a diagnosed intellectual disability, with five of the students also having diagnoses of autism spectrum disorder. It quickly became clear that this group of students struggled to transition from lunchtime social activities to a productive learning mode required for their curriculum work because of arguments and friendship issues. While I addressed major incidents with discussion and debriefing where needed, the twice-daily conflicts and dysregulation prevented them from settling into a routine quickly and began impacting curriculum responsibilities.

WHAT PROMPTED YOU TO PURSUE THE "REGULATION" PIECE?

After speaking with the school principal, she and I decided to try something proactive to support the students to settle after lunch breaks each day. I spent a week researching online in the evenings and putting together a plan for a low-impact yoga routine after the first break each day, and then using calming music as a settling tool after the second break each day.

WHY YOGA AND MUSIC (WITH THAT BAND)?

The principal at that school used yoga each morning to center her mind and body in preparation for work. I had also recently begun morning yoga to retain flexibility and fitness. We both thought it was worth a shot, and the research I did during that week uncovered a wealth of material from studies showing definite links between yoga and emotional regulation, so we decided to trial it for a few weeks and see how it went.

During my online research, I discovered a band named Marconi Union, who had worked with the British Academy of Sound Therapy to develop a track called "Weightless." They used scientific principles to create a musical track that was then used in a study and shown to reduce 65 percent of overall anxiety and 35 percent of psychological resting rates.[1]

We decided to try this song on an old iPod with headphones for a Year 8 boy who was very emotionally dysregulated while at school to see if we had positive results.

HOW DID THESE STRATEGIES IMPACT BEHAVIOR AND ACADEMIC PROGRESS?

First, the students were skeptical about taking off their shoes and sitting on the floor doing yoga. There were many jokes, laughs, and a few awkward moments, but we persevered. I was upfront with the students and explained why I wanted to try it. We talked about

---

[1] www.dancemusicnw.com/mindlab-study-song-macaroni-union-weightless-de-crease-anxiety

running a trial together for a week and then deciding if we would continue. The students agreed they would rather do this than do curriculum work, so they felt they were getting a good deal! I was willing to try anything to get consistently focused engagement in the first period after lunch, so I took the gamble that I could make up that ten minutes in the following 50 by not having to spend so much time on class management tasks.

The students very quickly began to see improvements in their mood. Those who came in feeling emotional or hurt were usually much calmer after yoga and ready to talk about what had happened. Those who came in feeling angry were usually much less angry after yoga and could then be negotiated with. I found myself looking forward to our ten minutes of yoga after the first break because it was a time when the class worked cohesively towards something and was happy most of the time. The students focused much better in the 50 minutes following the yoga activity. They were engaging better with the content, were more organized, more cognitively alert, and better at retaining skills from one day to the next.

The student struggling to regulate his emotions was also a success story. He was usually so upset on arrival at school that we set up a routine where he was moved into the classroom with a teacher or aide each morning. He rarely joined in with the class morning routine and learning activities; however, this changed once we introduced the Marconi Union track as an option. Most mornings, he would still come inside angry or sad. Instead of yelling and throwing items, he requested "his calming music," the Marconi Union track "Weightless." He would listen to the iPod for 20 minutes while doing a preferred activity or sitting on cushions at the back of the room and would then usually be ready to join the class when our morning routine began. Over time, the track became part of his strategy to self-regulate and gain more control over his day. He had initially presented himself as a student who was almost always angry. Still, with the yoga and "Weightless" track, he became a student who was able to verbally express when he needed space or was beginning to get angry and who would self-select his iPod and "calming music" as a strategy to calm himself when upset. One day, this student began to cry quietly toward the end of yoga. As the others packed up, I asked him if he was okay, and his response was truly beautiful. He said, "I'm crying because my heart feels clean now."

Both the teacher aide and I noticed such a marked improvement with this student and the entire group that yoga became a part of the classroom routine from then on.

Contributor: Lindy Anning

Children Learning to Independently Manage Behavior (C.L.I.M.B.)

C.L.I.M.B.ING OUT OF THE SUSPENSION CYCLE

In 2015, Mayflower Mill Elementary in Lafayette, Indiana, consciously decided to minimize out-of-school suspensions by creating a unique, alternative program allowing students to remain at school while receiving intensive social and emotional instruction in their areas of need.

At the time, aggressive, disruptive, and unsafe behaviors were pervasive in the building, and there was a high level of dysregulation in both students and staff. Our school had significantly high suspension rates. With no other options for students who reached the end of their traditional discipline ladder, we consistently suspended students who would predictably return to school unchanged. Well, that is untrue. When the students returned to school, one thing had *always* changed—their growing mistrust and lack of felt safety in our building. These students, who we knew lacked the skills to be successful, would instantly return to the same suspendable behaviors, leading to a repeated outcome. We were stuck in a traditional, punitive discipline cycle that was not helping students, teachers, or families. We knew we needed to make a change.

After consulting with educators at Allen Elementary School in Marion, Indiana, about New Beginnings, an alternative approach they created to change behavior, our principal, Shannon Cauble, and and I, a classroom teacher, created the C.L.I.M.B. program at Mayflower Mill Elementary School, becoming the second school in the state of Indiana to utilize an alternative to out-of-school suspension program for students at the elementary level. The program has evolved and grown in the eight years since its creation and it can now provide proactive interventions for students in Tier 2 in addition to the students in Tier 3 who are utilizing the C.L.I.M.B. alternative programming.

IDENTIFYING STUDENTS FOR THE C.L.I.M.B. PROGRAM

With the school-wide implementation of applied educational neuroscience and restorative practices, discipline at Mayflower Mill now looks very different. We now have many different options to develop discipline in our students with co-regulation, re-teaching, and repairing harm done. However, just as we see in academics, some students require more intensive, targeted intervention and ongoing support to see growth. For these students, receiving this instruction in Tier 1 is not enough. We continue to see behaviors escalate, become chronic, or simply so severe that the student requires some time out of the classroom. This is when a student may reach the point of suspension.

At Mayflower Mill, we believe the research that shows that out-of-school suspensions are ineffective and contribute to the school-to-prison pipeline (Thompson, n.d.). We recognize the need for struggling students to spend time outside their classroom to receive targeted support for their areas of need. At this time, parents can choose C.L.I.M.B. instead of an out-of-school suspension. Once a parent allows their child to start C.L.I.M.B., they participate in an intake meeting with me, as the C.L.I.M.B. classroom teacher.

PARENT INVOLVEMENT

Parent involvement is a requirement for students completing C.L.I.M.B. This begins with an initial intake meeting when a student starts the program for the school year. Parents meet in person with Jessica to learn about the program and the philosophy that drives it. These meetings are so important because, often, family members of students have had their own negative experiences with punitive discipline systems, and they must understand the restorative nature of the C.L.I.M.B. classroom. Parents are reassured that this is *not* a "scared straight" program. While students will be held to specific expectations, they will also receive support to make them successful, and love and positive reflection.

Each step of the program is explained to parents in detail and they are given a handbook to reference at home. At the end of each school day, the student takes home a daily communication report to share with their parents to help them understand how to see their child's progress. This also allows the child and parent to have meaningful conversations at home. The parent signs the report, and the student returns it each day. There is one more parent expectation that must always be explained and agreed on: parents understand that if their child has an ongoing safety concern or is unable to become regulated after an extended time, they will be asked to come in and support their child until they are safe, regulated, and operating in their cortex again. This is important because no child should ever think they can do anything "bad enough" for us to give up on them.

The C.L.I.M.B. philosophy works because we keep the students and work through every crisis, offering love to the child the entire time. We do not send them to the office. We do not send them home. We see each crisis through. But in severe situations, we recognize that we may not be enough to help the child feel safe. At that point, parents know they will be asked to come in and provide support until their child is in a regulated brain state, but they are never asked to take them home.

The response from participating parents is amazing! I receive text messages from parents checking in or giving me important information daily. I share my cell phone number with them and tell them, "If you are trusting me with your child, I can trust you with my cell phone number!" Parents appreciate that we are on the same team and are wonderfully supportive of our program.

LEVELED SYSTEM

C.L.I.M.B. is a leveled system. Students work restoratively to earn their way back into their classrooms full-time without support. To be very clear, the point and level system is *not* why students succeed in our classroom. The restorative work, the intentional behavior instruction, and the relationships between staff and students are why students succeed in this classroom. No student can acquire lagging skills due to offering positive points *or* the threat of losing points. The leveled point system is used strategically by C.L.I.M.B. staff to reinforce students positively and frequently enough. The point system is also used for students to gauge their proximity to their goal of returning to their classroom. Students are motivated to return to their classroom and deserve to know when that time is coming. Some students are anxious about returning to their larger classroom; this change needs to be predictable for these students.

TRANSITIONING BACK TO CLASS

Once students work through the C.L.I.M.B. program (on average, three to five days), they begin a transitional level consisting of two half-day class visits. On the half-day visit days, students spend the morning back in their classrooms, with support from a C.L.I.M.B. staff member. This serves several purposes:

- *It ensures a sense of felt safety:* Some students have anxiety about returning or can become overstimulated by the larger setting. Because the C.L.I.M.B. experience fosters close relationships with staff members, students feel more at ease and supported during these initial, sometimes precarious, moments of return to the classroom.

- *It provides "on-site" practice of strategies:* Students can practice learned replacement behaviors and coping strategies in their classroom during real moments of stress. Should they need additional support, a C.L.I.M.B. teacher is right there to coach them through the process while they work to use their new learning for authentic scenarios.

- *It offers a look at setting's conditions:* While supervising the C.L.I.M.B. student, the accompanying staff member has a unique opportunity to study the setting's conditions from the student's perspective. The C.L.I.M.B. teacher watches for challenging academic areas, noticeable triggers, and somato-sensory issues such as temperature, lighting, and volume, and the overall environment of the classroom. The C.L.I.M.B. teacher can use these observations to make suggestions to the classroom teacher for opportunities to adjust the classroom setting to be more conducive to the student's needs.

- *It fosters readiness/accountability:* If a student struggles during their half-day visit and is unable to be coached through the problem, it may be necessary to extend the child's time in C.L.I.M.B. to be able to continue to instruct in this targeted area. It is important to use aspects of restorative justice should the visit to class result in any harm done. A re-entry plan or circle may be used to ensure the student and the class feel ready to move forward.

EXIT MEETINGS

An exit meeting is scheduled before a student completes their two half-day visits and is ready to return to class independently. This meeting includes the classroom teacher, the C.L.I.M.B. teacher, and an administrator. At this meeting, either an ongoing support plan is created or a previously created plan is improved. Staff members understand that a new skill requires time and repetition. The child will return to class still in need of support. After all, we know we could not send a child struggling in reading to an interventionist for three days and expect them to read at grade level. Nor can we expect this from a child struggling with behavior. The team will look at all areas impacting the student and determine supports and interventions that can be implemented. The C.L.I.M.B. classroom can be accessed by the student for many of these supports.

ONGOING SUPPORT

When a child has completed C.L.I.M.B. and returns to their class-room, there are many ways for them to continue to access the C.L.I.M.B. classroom, staff, and programming. The C.L.I.M.B. class-room becomes a type of resource room for these students so they understand that they do not have to get into trouble to be able to return to this safe and smaller environment. They can access the classroom regularly, both scheduled and as needed. Some services the C.L.I.M.B. classroom provides to its "graduated" students include a breakfast club (soft start intervention), heart-rate monitor technology, access to the Calm Corner for regulation, check-in/check-out, hard resets (afternoon soft start intervention), mindfulness, Bal-A-Vis-X, and an alternate work environment.

TIER 2 SUPPORT/INTERVENTIONS

The C.L.I.M.B. program at Mayflower Mill Elementary has grown so much over time that now it is also able to serve students needing Tier 2 behavioral interventions. These are students who have not yet reached the suspension point. Still, they are struggling, and our goal is to identify them and begin working with them proactively to prevent them from ever needing to enter the C.L.I.M.B. program instead of suspension. These students are identified by teacher data or high levels of office referrals. Some Tier 2 supports students receive through behavior problem-solving include the breakfast club (soft start intervention), heart rate monitor technology, access to a Calm Corner for regulation, mindfulness, and Bal-A-Vis-X.

THE CHANGE WE SEE IN STUDENTS

The beauty of the C.L.I.M.B. program is that the students grow and change because of the combination of the priority placed on growth and character development, a high level of structure, and support provided with love and encouragement. We know students do not grow and change because they fear punitive consequences. Students feel at their very best in the C.L.I.M.B. classroom because it is set up to allow them to succeed. The students develop a deep trust with the C.L.I.M.B. teachers and feel comfortable utilizing the space for ongoing help. This is "suspension." This is "discipline." We are redefining these terms at Mayflower Mill Elementary. Children can feel loved, safe, special, *and* held accountable in ways that make sense and are based on teaching and learning, not fear and punishment.

Contributor: Jessica Harris

Personal, Professional, and Social Justice Journey Inventory

What I have come to understand in my...	Personal journey?	Professional journey?	Social justice journey?
	What do I realize?	What would be noticed?	What would be noticed?
Theories and mindsets about behavior and motivation	What aspects of my practice have been informed by behavioral science?	How does behaviorism show up in my classroom?	How does behaviorism show up in school policy and practices?
Intrinsic motivation conditions (i.e., autonomy, competence, and relatedness)	What aspects of how I go about the work I do reflect these three conditions? How does it feel for me?	How am I building these conditions into my planning and delivery? How are students reacting to my encouragement of self-directed motivation?	What larger projects are developing these conditions across the school population? How am I helping?
The basics of brain structure and function	What has happened to me and my brain during my life? What is happening now?	What do I better understand about brain development in children and adolescents?	What do injustice, inequity, and discrimination do to the way brains develop and function? What am I seeing?

cont.

What I have come to understand in my...	Personal journey? What do I realize?	Professional journey? What would be noticed?	Social justice journey? What would be noticed?
Fight, flight, or freeze behaviors	What responses of my own show up in my stress responses? Am I aware of my own activators?	What am I now seeing in individual and classroom behaviors that I can better understand through brain science?	Through the lens of school policy and practice, how does the school view and respond to fight, fight, or freeze behaviors?
Becoming aware of triggers that influence behavior	What makes me feel safe or unsafe?	What do I see affecting a sense of safety for my students? How do I know when they feel safe or unsafe?	What issues in general trigger whole-school community dysregulation?
My nervous system has cues that activate it	What do students do that activates my system? Can I work on those responses?	What sorts of issues in my classroom activate students' nervous systems?	What recent specific issues and/or incidents have caused upheaval?
My nervous system state is contagious	How am I staying regulated, so I have it to share?	How am I sharing my state? Is it positive or negative?	How am I offering calm to others in my community?
Implicit bias— hiding in plain sight	What have I discovered about myself and about the biases I have? How has this impacted my behavior and challenged my connections?	How does bias show up in my classroom? What feedback would my students offer me if I asked?	How does bias show up in my school's policy, especially around disciplinary matters?

Relational approaches to problem-solving	Am I using a range of restorative options that reflect my understanding and commitment to humanistic approaches to relational education?	Am I working to connect my students with each other, promoting kindness and collaboration?	Has my school embarked on a path of culture change to develop awareness, and change mindsets and practices that reflect the value of relationships? Am I contributing?
Connecting	Do I understand what really matters to my learners? Do they feel connected to me?	Do I greet and welcome my students at the door and find out how ready they are for learning?	Do I extend this relationship development work to my colleagues and the parents?
Modeling	Am I prepared to model the behaviors I want to see? Which of these do I need to develop?	Are my students starting to show how my modeling is having an impact?	Am I showing up in school meetings and professional development sessions willing to model these preferred behaviors? Do I speak up? Do I encourage the voice of others?
Regulating and co-regulating	Can I tell when I need to settle myself? I must regulate my own brain first.	Do I have routines in place that help individuals and the whole class to settle, ready for learning, and strategies to help those students who are still struggling?	Is our whole school committed to the ideas and practices of regulation and co-regulation? Is there is a coherent approach to achieve this? What would be seen?

cont.

What I have come to understand in my...	*Personal journey?* What do I realize?	*Professional journey?* What would be noticed?	*Social justice journey?* What would be noticed?
Movement is regulating	Am I getting enough movement in the day to keep me regulated?	Are my students getting enough movement?	Are there regulating activities into the school culture?
Attending to wellness	Am I paying attention to the needs of my body and brain health?	Am I aware of how healthy my relationships are with my colleagues? If unhealed ruptures exist involving me, am I prepared to work on them?	Is our whole school community characterized by trusting and mutually respectful relationships? Is this a key value that guides decisions?
Impact of trauma on the brain and behavior	Do I have a better understanding now of how stress and any trauma have impacted me?	Do I understand the backgrounds of my students so that I can view their behavior through a trauma-informed lens and respond in ways that settle and connect with them?	Does the school understand that trauma comes in all shapes and sizes; that its policies, practices, and structures can cause more harm? Is our school seeking to minimize these harms?

Understanding the impact of shame	What shames me? How do I respond when that happens?	How do I minimize unnecessary shame in my classroom? What behaviors of mine have I committed to changing?	Have we as a whole community identified the policies, structures, and practices that shame children and adults? Are we committed to minimizing the likelihood of intentionally shaming our community?
The six elements of positive developmental and educational settings (the six Rs)	Do my lessons meet any of the six elements?	Are my students connecting to me as an educator? And to the lesson I am teaching?	Is respect the underlying space for my lessons?
This work is intentional	How am I setting myself up to be trauma-informed and restorative?	How am I setting up my classroom to be trauma-informed and restorative?	How am I intentionally addressing issues of injustice in my community?

References

Abramson, L. C. (2014). Being Emotional, Being Human: Creating Communities and Institutions by Honoring our Biology. In V. C. Kelly & M. Thorsborne (eds), *The Psychology of Emotion in Restorative Practice: How Affect Script Psychology Explains How and Why Restorative Practice Works* (pp.84–104). London: Jessica Kingsley Publishers.

Abramson, L. & Beck, E. (2011). Using Conflict to Build Community: Community Conferencing. In E. Beck, N. P. Kropf, & P. B. Leonard (eds), *Social Work and Restorative Justice: Skills for Dialogue, Peacemaking, and Reconciliation* (pp.149–174). New York, NY: Oxford University Press.

Adams, D. (2017). *The Hitchhiker's Guide to the Galaxy*. New York, NY: Del Ray.

Alexander, B. K., Beyerstein, B. L., Hadaway, B. F., & Coombs, R. B. (1981). Effect of early and later colony housing on oral ingestion of morphine in rats. *Pharmacology Biochemistry and Behavior*, 15, 571–576.

Aliaksei, P. (2020, December). Trust in Ultima Thules: Social capital and renewable energy development in Iceland and Greenland. Part I. *Artic and North*, 41(41), 182–219. Retrieved from www.researchgate.net/publication/347996295_Trust_in_Ultima_Thules_Social_Capital_and_Renewable_Energy_Development_in_Iceland_and_Greenland_Part_I.

American Academy of Sleep Medicine. (2016). *What you eat can influence how you sleep: Daily intake of fiber, saturated fat and sugar may impact sleep quality.* Retrieved from www.sciencedaily.com/releases/2016/01/160114213443.htm.

American Medical Association. (2023). *AMA House of Delegates Handbook (2023 Annual Meeting)*. American Medical Association. Retrieved from www.ama-assn.org/system/files/a23-combined-handbook.pdf.

American Psychological Association. (2023a). *APA Dictionary of Psychology*. Retrieved from https://dictionary.apa.org/stressor.

American Psychological Association (2023b, March 8). *Stress Effects on the Body*. Retrieved from www.apa.org/topics/stress#.

Arvidsson, I., Hakansson, C., Karlson, B., Bjork, J., *et al.* (2016). Burnout among Swedish school teachers: A cross-sectional analysis. *BMC Public Health*, 16(823). https://doi.org/10.1186/s12889-016-3498-7.

Australian Institute of Health and Welfare. (2021, June 25). *Australia's youth: COVID-19 and the impact on young people*. Retrieved from www.aihw.gov.au/reports/children-youth/covid-19-and-young-people#.

Badenoch, B. (2018). *The Heart of Trauma*. New York, NY: Norton Publishing.

Barrett, L. F. (2017). *How Emotions are Made: The Secret Life of the Brain*. Boston, MA: Mariner.

Barrett, L. F. (2023, April 26). *That is not how your brain works*. Big Think. Retrieved from https://bigthink.com/neuropsych/not-how-your-brain-works.

Bauer, J., Stamm, A., Virnich, K., Wissing, K., *et al.* (2006). Correlation between burnout syndrome and psychological and psychosomatic symptoms among teachers. *International Archives of Occupational and Environmental Health*, 79(3), 199–204. https://doi.org/10.1007/s00420-005-0050-y.

Bishop, S. R., Lau, M., Shapiro, S., Carlson, L., *et al.* (2004). Mindfulness: A proposed operational definition. *Clinical Psychology: Science and Practice*, 11(3), 230–241. https://doi.org/10.1093/clipsy.bph077.

Boyes-Watson, C. & Pranis, K. (2015). *Circle Forward: Building a Restorative School Community*. St. Paul, MN: Living Justice Press.

Braithwaite, J. (1989). *Crime, Shame and Reintegration*. Cambridge: Cambridge University Press.

Brighouse, T. & Waters, M. (2021). *About Our Schools: Improving on Previous Best*. Bancyfelin, Carmarthen: Crown House Publishing.

Briguglio, M., Dell'Osso, B., Panzica, G., Malgaroli, A., *et al.* (2018). Dietary neurotransmitters: A narrative review on current knowledge. *Nutrients*, 10(5), 591. doi: 10.3390/nu10050591. Retrieved from www.ncbi.nlm.nih.gov/pmc/articles/PMC5986471.

Brown, B. (2021). *Atlas of the Heart: Mapping Meaningful Connection and the Language of Human Experience*. New York, NY: Random House.

Brown, G. S. (2022). *The Self-Healing Mind: An Essential Five-Step Practice for Overcoming Anxiety and Depression, and Revitalizing Your Life*. New York, NY: Harper.

Brummer, J. & Thorsborne, M. (2020). *Building a Trauma-Informed Restorative School: Skills and Approaches for Improving Culture and Behavior*. London: Jessica Kingsley Publishers.

Centre for YouthAOD Practice Development. (n.d.). *The Out of Home Care Toolbox*. Retrieved from www.oohctoolbox.org.au/trauma-and-memory.

Conti, P. (2021). *Trauma: The Invisible Epidemic: How Trauma Works and How We Can Heal From It*. Boulder, CO: Sounds True.

Comana, F. (2022). *Non-exercise activity thermogenesis: A neat approach to weight loss*. Retrieved from https://blog.nasm.org/exercise-programming/neat-approach-weight-loss.

Coulson, J. (2023). *The Parenting Revolution: The Guide to Raising Resilient Kids*. Sydney, NSW: ABC Books.

Cozolino, L. J. (2014). *The Neuroscience of Human Relationships: Attachment and the Developing Social Brain*. New York, NY: W.W. Norton & Company.

Dana, D. (2020). *Polyvagal Flip Chart: Understanding the Science of Safety*. New York, NY: W.W. Norton & Company.

Darwin, C. (1873). *The Expression of the Emotions in Man and Animals: With Photographic and Other Illustrations*. London: Murray.

Demos, E. V. (2019). *The Affect Theory of Silvan Tomkins for Psychoanalysis and Psychotherapy: Recasting the Essentials*. Abingdon, Oxon: Routledge.

Desautels, L. L. (2020). *Connections Over Compliance: Rewiring Our Perceptions of Discipline*. Deadwood, OR: Wyatt-MacKenzie Publishing.

Desautels, L. L. (2022, September 10–11). *"Behaviour" is more than meets the eye: Looking through the lens of the nervous system!* 2022 Trauma Aware Schooling Conference, Brisbane, Australia [Conference presentation, Keynote address]. Retrieved from www.traumaawareeducation.com.au/wp-content/uploads/2022/06/TAS-2022-program-grid_v5.pdf.

Desautels, L. L. (2023). *Intentional Neuroplasticity: Moving Our Nervous Systems and Educational System Toward Post-Traumatic Growth.* Deadwood, OR: Wyatt-MacKenzie Publishing.

Desautels, L. L. & McKnight, M. (2019). *Eyes Are Never Quiet: Listening Beneath the Behaviors of Our Most Troubled Students.* Deadwood, OR: Wyatt-MacKenzie Publishing.

de Sousa, F., Ordônio, M. S., Santos, T. F., Santos, G. C. J., *et al.* (2020, December 20). Effects of physical exercise on neuroplasticity and brain function: A systematic review in human and animal studies. *Neural Plasticity.* Retrieved from https://doi.org/10.1155/2020/8856621.

Dolezal, L. & Gibson, M. (2022). Beyond a trauma-informed approach and towards shame-sensitive practice. *Humanities and Social Sciences Communications,* 9(214). doi:10.1057/s41599-022-01227-z.

Doucleff, M. (2021). *Hunt, Gather, Parent: What Ancient Cultures Can Teach Us About the Lost Art of Raising Happy, Helpful Little Humans.* New York, NY: Avid Reader Press.

Evans, K. & Vaandering, D. (2022) *The Little Book of Restorative Justice in Education: Fostering Responsibility, Healing, and Hope in Schools.* New York, NY: Good Books.

Fandakova, Y. & Hartley, C. A. (2020). Mechanisms of learning and plasticity in childhood and adolescence. *Developmental Cognitive Neuroscience,* 42. Retrieved from https://doi.org/10.1016/j.dcn.2020.100764.

Farese, G. M. (2016). The cultural semantics of the Japanese emotion terms "Haji" and "Hazukashii." *New Voices in Japanese Studies,* 8, 32–54. Retrieved from https://doi.org/10.21159/nvjs.08.02.

Finnis, M. (2021). *Independent Thinking on Restorative Practice: Building Relationships, Improving Behaviour and Creating Stronger Communities.* Bancyfelin, Carmarthen, Wales: Independent Thinking Press.

Freeman, S. (2015, January 1). *Honour/Shame Dynamics in Sub-Saharan Africa.* Retrieved from www.missionfrontiers.org/issue/article/honour-shame-dynamics-in-sub-saharan-africa.

George. G. (2014). Affect and Emotion in a Restorative School. In V. C. Kelly & M. Thorsborne (eds), *The Psychology of Emotion in Restorative Practice: How Affect Script Psychology Explains How and Why Restorative Practice Works* (pp.200–232). London: Jessica Kingsley Publishers.

Giedd, J. N. (2016). Risky teen behavior is driven by an imbalance in brain development. *Scientific American,* 312(6), 32–37. Retrieved from www.scientificamerican.com/article/risky-teen-behavior-is-driven-by-an-imbalance-in-brain-development.

Gonzalez, M. J. & Miranda-Massari, J. R. (2014). Diet and stress. *Psychiatric Clinics of North America,* 37, 579–589. Retrieved from www.researchgate.net/publication/265645052_Diet_and_Stress.

Graner, S. & Perry, B. D. (2023). *Translating the six R's for the educational setting.* (Revised from A "6Rs" translational template for educators, 2020). Houston, TX: NMN Press.

Greene, R. W. (2014). *Lost at School: Why Our Kids with Behavioral Challenges Are Falling Through the Cracks and How We Can Help Them.* New York, NY: Scribner.

Greene, R. W. (2021). *Lost and Found: Unlocking Collaboration and Compassion to Help Our Most Vulnerable, Misunderstood Students (And All The Rest)* (second edition). Hoboken, NJ: Jossey-Bass.

Greenberg, M. T., Brown J. L., & Abenavoli, R.M. (2016). *Teacher Stress and Health Effects on Teachers, Students, and Schools.* Edna Bennett Pierce Prevention

Research Center, Pennsylvania State University. Retrieved from https://prevention.psu.edu/wp-content/uploads/2022/09/rwjf430428-TeacherStress.pdf.

Hansberry, W. (2016). *A Practical Introduction to Restorative Practice in Schools: Theory, Skills and Guidance.* London: Jessica Kingsley Publishers.

Harkins, J. (1990). Shame and shyness in the Aboriginal classroom: A case for "practical semantics." *Australian Journal of Linguistics,* 10(2), 293–306. doi: 10.1080/07268609008599445.

Harvard University. (2011). *Healthy Eating Plate.* Retrieved from www.hsph.harvard.edu/nutritionsource/healthy-eating-plate.

Harvard University. (2023, August). *Processed Foods and Health.* Retrieved from www.hsph.harvard.edu/nutritionsource/processed-foods.

Health and Social Care Information Centre. (2022). *Mental health of children and young people in England 2022—Wave 3 follow up to the 2017 survey.* Retrieved from https://digital.nhs.uk/data-and-information/publications/statistical/mental-health-of-children-and-young-people-in-england/2022-follow-up-to-the-2017-survey.

Healy, G. (2023). *Regulation and Co-regulation: Accessible Neuroscience and Connection strategies that Bring Calm into the Classroom.* Chattanooga, TN: National Center for Youth Issues.

Holinger, P. C. (2018, November 5). *Understanding bias and prejudice—and violence: Curiosity about novelty vs. distress, anger, and fear of differences.* Retrieved from www.psychologytoday.com/us/blog/great-kids-great-parents/201811/understanding-bias-and-prejudice-and-violence.

Holinger, P. C. (2022, June 30). The role of affects in bias, prejudice, and violence: Early negative feelings can supply the fuel for later bias and violence. *Psychology Today.* Retrieved from www.psychologytoday.com/us/blog/great-kids-great-parents/202206/the-role-affects-in-bias-prejudice-and-violence.

Holinger, P. C. & Doner, K. (2003). *What Babies Say Before They Can Talk: The Nine Signals Infants Use to Express Their Feelings.* New York, NY: Fireside.

Holt, L. & Murray, L. (2021). Children and Covid 19 in the UK. *Children's Geographies,* 20(4), 487–494. Retrieved from https://doi.org/10.1080/14733285.2021.1921699.

Horvath, E. (2023). New insights on brain development sequence through adolescence. *Neuroscience News.* Retrieved from https://neurosciencenews.com/adolescent-brain-plasticity-22972.

Howard, J. A. (2022). *Trauma-Aware Education: Essential Information and Guidance for Educators, Education Sites and Education Systems.* Samford Valley: Australian Academic Press.

Huberman, A. (2022, June 6). *Dr. Paul Conti: Therapy, Treating Trauma & Other Life Challenges* [Audio podcast episode 75]. In Huberman Lab. Retrieved from www.youtube.com/watch?v=IOl28gj_RXw.

Huppert, F. A. (2009). Psychological well-being: Evidence regarding its causes and consequences. *Applied Psychology: Health and Well-being,* 1(2), 137–164. doi:10.1111/j.1758-0854.2009.01008.x.

Institute of Medicine. (2006). *Sleep Disorders and Sleep Deprivation: An Unmet Public Health Problem.* Washington, DC: The National Academies Press. Retrieved from https://doi.org/10.17226/11617.

Karbowski, D. (2022, April 12). *The State of Teaching 2022.* Retrieved from www.adoptaclassroom.org/2022/04/12/state-of-teaching-statistics-2022.

Karp, D. R. & Armour, M. (2019). *The Little Book of Restorative Justice for Colleges and Universities: Repairing Harm and Rebuilding Trust in Response to Student Misconduct.* New York, NY: Good Books.

Kelly, V. C. (2014a). Caring, Restorative Practice and the Biology of Emotion. In V. C. Kelly & M. Thorsborne (eds), *The Psychology of Emotion in Restorative Practice: How Affect Script Psychology Explains How and Why Restorative Practice Works* (pp.26–53). London: Jessica Kingsley Publishers.

Kelly, V. C. (2014b). Interpersonal Caring, Social Discipline, and a Blueprint for Restorative Healing. In V. C. Kelly & M. Thorsborne (eds), *The Psychology of Emotion in Restorative Practice: How Affect Script Psychology Explains How and Why Restorative Practice Works* (pp.54–82). London: Jessica Kingsley Publishers.

Kelly, W. (2017). *Understanding Children in Foster Care: Identifying and Addressing What Children Learn From Maltreatment.* Cham, Switzerland: Palgrave Macmillan.

Kelly, V. C. & Lamia, M. C. (2018). *The Upside of Shame: Therapeutic Interventions Using the Positive Aspects of a "Negative" Emotion.* New York, NY: W.W. Norton & Company.

Kim, R. M. & Venet, A. S. (2023). Unsnarling PBIS and trauma-informed education. *Urban Education.* Retrieved from https://doi.org/10.1177/00420859231175670.

Kohn, A. (1993, 1999, 2018). *Punished by Rewards: The Trouble with Gold Stars, Incentive Plans, A's, Praise, and Other Bribes.* Boston, MA: Mariner Books.

Lebrun-Harris, L. A., Ghandour, R. M., Kogan, M. D., & Warren, M. D. (2022). Five-year trends in US children's health and well-being, 2016-2020. *AMA Pediatrics,* 176(7). doi:10.1001/jamapediatrics.2022.0056.

Lemov, D. (2021). *Teach Like a Champion 3.0: 63 Techniques that Put Students on the Path to College.* Hoboken, NJ: John Wiley & Sons.

Lemov, D., Lewis, H., Williams, D., & Frazier, D., (2023). *Reconnect: Building School Culture for Meaning, Purpose, and Belonging.* Hoboken, NJ: Jossey-Bass.

Lombardi, V. (n.d.). Vince Lombardi Quotes. Retrieved from www.brainyquote.com/quotes/vince_lombardi_138158.

McShane, E. P. (2020). *Conquering Trauma and Anxiety to Find Happiness.* New York, NY: Peter Lang.

Malcolm, L. (Host). (2018, December 30). *Carrots, sticks...and other ways to motivate.* Retrieved from www.abc.net.au/listen/programs/allinthemind/carrots,-sticks-...-and-other-ways-to-motivate/10571878.

Marshall, C. (n.d.). *Knowledge seminar: Restorative practices in schools* [Support material]. Retrieved from https://pb4l.tki.org.nz/PB4L-Restorative-Practice/Support-material.

Maté, G., & Maté, D. (2022). *The Myth of Normal: Trauma, Illness, and Healing in a Toxic Culture.* New York, NY: Penguin.

Mission Australia. (2022). *Mission Australia, Youth Survey 2022.* Retrieved from www.missionaustralia.com.au/publications/youth-survey.

Monteiro, C. A., Cannon, G., Levy, R., Moubarac, J. C., *et al.* (2016, January 7). NOVA. The star shines bright. [Food classification. Public health]. *World Nutrition,* 7(1–3). Retrieved from https://worldnutritionjournal.org/index.php/wn/article/view/5/4.

Munro, C. L. & Savel, R. H. (2016, May 1). Narrowing the 17-year research to practice gap. *American Journal of Critical Care,* 25(3), 194–196. Retrieved from https://aacnjournals.org/ajcconline/article/25/3/194/3121/Narrowing-the-17-Year-Research-to-Practice-Gap.

Nagoski, E. & Nagoski, A. (2020). *Burnout: The Secret to Unlocking the Stress Cycle.* New York, NY: Ballantine Books.

Nathanson, D. L. (1992). *Shame and Pride: Affect, Sex, and the Birth of the Self.* New York, NY: W.W. Norton & Company.

National Heart, Blood, and Lung Institute. (2022, March 24). *What are sleep deprivation and deficiency?* Retrieved from www.nhlbi.nih.gov/health/sleep-deprivation.

National Scientific Council on the Developing Child. (2015). *Supportive relationships and active skill-building strengthen the foundations of resilience: Working paper No. 13.* Retrieved from www.developingchild.harvard.edu.

National Sleep Foundation. (2020, October 1). *How much sleep do you really need?* Retrieved from www.thensf.org/how-many-hours-of-sleep-do-you-really-need.

National Wellness Institute. (2023). *What is wellness?* Retrieved from https://nationalwellness.org/resources/six-dimensions-of-wellness.

Neurosequential Network. (n.d.). *Neurosequential Model in Education.* Retrieved from www.neurosequential.com/nme.

Oberg, C., Hodges, H. R., Gander, S., Nathawad, R., *et al.* (2022). The impact of COVID-19 on children's lives in the United States: Amplified inequities and a just path to recovery. *Current Problems in Pediatric and Adolescent Healthcare,* 52(7). Retrieved from www.ncbi.nlm.nih.gov/pmc/articles/PMC8923900.

Office of the US Surgeon General. (2023). *Our Epidemic of Loneliness and Isolation: The U.S. Surgeon General's Advisory on the Healing Effects of Social Connection and Community.* Retrieved from www.hhs.gov/sites/default/files/surgeon-general-social-connection-advisory.pdf.

Perry, B. D. (2006). Applying Principles of Neuroscience to Clinical Work with Traumatized and Maltreated Children: The Neurosequential Model of Therapeutics. In N. B. Webb (ed.), *Working with Traumatized Youth in Child Welfare* (pp.27–52). New York: NY: The Guilford Press.

Perry, B. D. (2020, August 25). *Stress, Trauma, and the Brain: Insights for Educators—The Neurosequential Model: How Stress Impacts Brain Function, Episode 2* [Video]. Retrieved from www.youtube.com/watch?v=_3is_3XHKKs.

Perry, B. D. & Szalavitz, M. (2006, 2017). *The Boy Who Was Raised as a Dog: And Other Stories from a Child Psychiatrist's Notebook—What Traumatized Children Can Teach Us About Loss, Love, and Healing.* New York, NY: Basic Books.

Perry, B. D. & Winfrey, O. (2021). *What Happened to You? Conversations on Trauma, Resilience, and Healing.* New York, NY: Flatiron.

Pink, D. H. (2009). *Drive: The Surprising Truth About What Motivates Us.* New York, NY: Penguin/Random House.

Porges, S. W. (2017). *The Pocket Guide to Polyvagal Theory: The Transformative Power of Feeling Safe.* New York, NY: W.W Norton & Company.

Porges, P. (2021, August 18). How Social Connection Combats Stress, Finding Mastery, Episode 290, Retrieved from https://findingmasyery.net/stephen-porges.

Qiu, J. & Morales-Muñoz, I. (2022). Associations between sleep and mental health in adolescents: Results from the UK millennium cohort study. *International Journal of Environmental Research and Public Health,* 19(3). doi:10.3390/ijerph19031868.

Reisel, D. (2013, February). *The Neuroscience of Restorative Justice.* [Video]. TED Conferences. Retrieved from www.ted.com/talks/dan_reisel_the_neuroscience_of_restorative_justice.

Reisel, D. (2015). Towards a Neuroscience of Morality. In T. Gavrielides (ed.), *The Psychology of Restorative Justice: Managing the Power Within* (pp.49–64). New York, NY: Routledge.

Roozendaal, B., McEwen, B., & Chatterjee, S. (2009). Stress, memory, and the amygdala. *Nature Reviews Neuroscience*, 10(6), 423–433.

Rosenberg, M. (2015). *Nonviolent Communication: A Language of Life* (third edition). Encinitas, CA: PuddleDancer Press.

Ruggeri, K., Garcia-Garzon, E., Maguire, A., Matz, S., *et al.* (2020). Well-being is more than happiness and life satisfaction: A multidimensional analysis of 21 countries. *Health and Quality of Life Outcomes*, 18(192), 1–16. Retrieved from https://doi.org/10.1186/s12955-020-01423-y.

Ryan, R. & Deci, E. (2020). Intrinsic and extrinsic motivation from a self-determination theory perspective: Definitions, theory, practices, and future directions. *Contemporary Educational Psychology*, 61. Retrieved from https://selfdeterminationtheory.org/wp-content/uploads/2020/04/2020_RyanDeci_CEP_PrePrint.pdf.

Sederer, L. L. (2019, June 10). What does "rat park" teach us about addiction? *Psychiatric Times*. Retrieved from www.psychiatrictimes.com/view/what-does-rat-park-teach-us-about-addiction.

Shanker, S. D. & Barker, T. (2017). *Self-Reg: How to Help Your Child (and You) Break the Stress Cycle and Successfully Engage with Life*. New York, NY: Penguin.

Shi, Z. (2019). Gut microbiota: An important link between western diet and chronic diseases. *Nutrients*, 11(10), 2287. Retrieved from www.ncbi.nlm.nih.gov/pmc/articles/PMC6835660/pdf/nutrients-11-02287.pdf.

Siegel, D. J. (2020). *The Developing Mind: How Relationships and the Brain Interact to Shape Who We Are*. New York, NY: The Guilford Press.

Singh, S., Yadav, N., & Jain, S. (2019). Sleep and health—An introduction. *International Journal of Head and Neck Surgery*, 10(1). Retrieved from www.ijhns.com/doi/IJHNS/pdf/10.5005/jp-journals-10001-1361.

Sleep Foundation. (2022, December 15). *How much sleep should a teenager get?* Retrieved from www.sleepfoundation.org/teens-and-sleep/how-much-sleep-does-a-teenager-need.

Smith, K. (2023, April 26). *Trauma is trauma: A mental health talk with Kevin Smith*. Retrieved from www.youtube.com/watch?v=JBvc7Ny4iUk.

Smith, D. O., Fisher, D., & Frey, N. (2022). *The Restorative Practices Playbook: Tools for Transforming Discipline in Schools*. Thousand Oaks, CA: Corwin Press.

Sominsky, L. & Spencer, S. J. (2014). Eating behavior and stress: A pathway to obesity. *Frontiers in Psychology*, 13(5). doi:10.3389/fpsyg.2014.00434.

Sorrels, B. (2015). *Reaching and Teaching Children Exposed to Trauma*. Lewisville, NC: Gryphon House.

Stephens, T. (2020, July 13). *Whakamā: Fighting the taniwha of shame*. Retrieved from https://thespinoff.co.nz/atea/13-07-2020/whakama-fighting-the-taniwha-of-shame.

Stone, D. M., Mack, K. A., & Qualters J. (2023, February 10). Notes from the field: Recent changes in suicide rates, by race and ethnicity and age group—United States, 2021. *Morbidity and Mortality Weekly Report*, 72(6), 160–162. doi: http://dx.doi.org/10.15585/mmwr.mm7206a4.

Stoner, S. & Stoner, H. H. (2018). *Adult Wellness Circle Program Workbook*. Retrieved from www.wellnesscompass.org.

Stowe, M. (2023). *Words Can Be Windows or Walls (Rosenberg)*. Retrieved from www.connectrp.ie/words-can-be-windows-or-walls-rosenberg.

Street, H. (2023, August). *Finding Motivation to Do Hard Things*. Retrieved from www.helenstreet.com/finding-motivation-to-do-hard-things-by-dr-helen-street.

Substance Abuse and Mental Health Services Administration. (2014). *SAMHSA's Concept of Trauma and Guidance for a Trauma-Informed Approach*. HHS Publication No. (SMA) 14-4884. Rockville, MD: Substance Abuse and Mental Health Services Administration. Retrieved from https://ncsacw.acf.hhs.gov/userfiles/files/SAMHSA_Trauma.pdf.

Thompson, H. (n.d.). Explaining the preschool-to-prison pipeline and ways to prevent it. Retrieved from https://eduequityforall.com/preschool-to-prison-pipeline-explained.

Thorsborne, M. (in press). *Restorative Practice in Australian Schools: Where Are We At?* Oceana Volume of the Encyclopedia of Restorative Justice.

Thorsborne, M. & Vinegrad, D. (2022). *The Continuum of Restorative Practices in Schools: An Instructional Training Manual for Practitioners*. London: Jessica Kingsley Publishers.

Tomkins, S. S. & Demos, E. V. (1995). *Exploring Affect: The Selected Writings of Silvan S Tomkins (Studies in Emotion and Social Interaction)*. Cambridge, England: Cambridge University Press.

Travis, J. W. & Ryan, R. S. (2004). *Wellness Workbook. How to Achieve Enduring Health and Vitality* (third edition.). New York, NY: Ten Speed Press.

van der Kolk, B. (2014). *The Body Keeps the Score: Brain, Mind, and Body in the Healing of Trauma*. New York, NY: Penguin.

Van Duijvenvoorde, A. C. K. & Crone, E. A. (2013). The teenage brain: A neuro-economic approach to adolescent decision making. *Current Directions in Psychological Science*, 22(2) 108–113. Retrieved from https://journals.sagepub.com/doi/pdf/10.1177/0963721413475446.

Venet, A. S. (2021, January 21). *Problematizing PBIS: Resource round-up*. Retrieved from https://unconditionallearning.org/2021/01/21/problematizing-pbis-resource-round-up.

Vora, E. (2022). *The Anatomy of Anxiety: Understanding and Overcoming the Body's Fear Response*. New York, NY: Harper.

Wachtel, T. (1999). *Restorative Justice in Everyday Life: Beyond the Formal Ritual*. Paper presented at the "Reshaping Australian Institutions Conference: Restorative Justice and Civil Society," Australian National University.

Walker, M. (2017). *Why We Sleep: Unlocking the Power of Sleep and Dreams*. New York, NY: Scribner.

Wilson, D. M. (2023). *Polyvagal Path to Joyful Learning: Transforming Classrooms One Nervous System at a Time*. New York, NY: W.W. Norton & Company.

Winfrey, O. (2013, March 24). *Shame is Lethal*. Oprah Winfrey Network. Retrieved from www.oprah.com/own-super-soul-sunday/dr-brene-brown-shame-is-lethal-video.

Zehr, H. (1990). *Changing Lenses: A New Focus for Crime and Justice (Christian Peace Shelf Selection)*. Harrisonburg, VA: Herald Press.

Zehr, H. (2015). *The Little Book of Restorative Justice*. New York, NY: Skyhorse.

Index